THE GOLD
OF THE GODS

By Erich von Daniken

Introduction by
David Hatcher Childress

Adventures Unlimited Press

Other Books by David Hatcher Childress:

VIMANA
ARK OF GOD
ANCIENT TECHNOLOGY IN PERU & BOLIVIA
THE MYSTERY OF THE OLMECS
PIRATES AND THE LOST TEMPLAR FLEET
TECHNOLOGY OF THE GODS
A HITCHHIKER'S GUIDE TO ARMAGEDDON
LOST CONTINENTS & THE HOLLOW EARTH
ATLANTIS & THE POWER SYSTEM OF THE GODS
THE FANTASTIC INVENTIONS OF NIKOLA TESLA
LOST CITIES OF NORTH & CENTRAL AMERICA
LOST CITIES OF CHINA, CENTRAL ASIA & INDIA
LOST CITIES & ANCIENT MYSTERIES OF AFRICA & ARABIA
LOST CITIES & ANCIENT MYSTERIES OF SOUTH AMERICA
LOST CITIES OF ANCIENT LEMURIA & THE PACIFIC
LOST CITIES OF ATLANTIS, ANCIENT EUROPE & THE MEDITERRANEAN
LOST CITIES & ANCIENT MYSTERIES OF THE SOUTHWEST
YETIS, SASQUATCH AND HAIRY GIANTS

With Brien Foerster
THE ENIGMA OF CRANIAL DEFORMATION

With Steven Mehler
THE CRYSTAL SKULLS

THE GOLD
OF THE GODS

By Erich von Daniken

Introduction by
David Hatcher Childress

Adventures Unlimited Press

TABLE OF CONTENTS

Introduction by David Hatcher Childress

In 1974 I was a high school student in Missoula, Montana. I worked afternoons and evenings at a supermarket where I bagged groceries, swept the floor and stocked shelves. This grocery store, like most at that time, had a rack of paperback books next to the magazines. In this rack I discovered a copy of *The Gold of the Gods* and bought it. I had heard of Erich before and had read *Chariots of the Gods* and seen the film. When I got home I eagerly read the book and stared at the photos.

I was not disappointed. Here was a tale of a gigantic megalithic city on a remote Pacific Island and also of a tunnel system in South America with a fantastic metal library! Wow, this was the sort of Indiana Jones adventure I had dreamed of as a teenager. The Indiana Jones movies were not to come for another decade and I soon left the United States and flew to Japan, Taiwan, Hong Kong, Bangkok, India and Nepal to begin my many years of traveling through Asia and Africa.

After that I made it to the megalithic sites in South America and to the amazing megalithic city called Nan Madol on the Micronesian island of Pohnpei. Erich's books were among the many books I read on ancient astronauts, Atlantis, and ancient technology. I got to meet Erich several times and even visited him at his Mystery Park in Switzerland at his invitation. This park is now closed.

I think that *The Gold of the Gods* is Erich's most interesting—and controversial—book. While he laid out his general philosophy of gods from outer space in his first couple of books, it was *The Gold of the Gods* that made a large number of people wonder if god really was an astronaut.

According to Erich von Däniken's organization, the books in his series have been translated into 32 languages and have sold more than 63 million copies. While we were on a three-week lecture tour in Australia, I got some personal background. He told me once over dinner that he had gone to a Catholic boarding school in Switzerland in the early 1950s and had a close friend who was a student from Egypt. That student invited him to visit him in Cairo. There, Erich was amazed at the temples and pyramids, and began to wonder about extraterrestrials and ancient civilizations. At 19 he began to travel as much as he could and worked in the hotel industry. He began working on his thesis in 1964 and his first book was finally published in Germany in 1968.

Erich has known some scandal, particularly one surrounding the book *The Gold of the Gods*, where von Däniken describes an expedition that he undertook through man-made tunnels within the Tayos Caves, a natural cave system in Ecuador. He says he was guided by a local man named Juan Moricz. He reported seeing mounds of gold, strange statues, and a library containing metal tablets, all of which he considered to be evidence of ancient extraterrestrial visitation. Erich also mentions a local priest, Father Crespi, who had stewardship of a collection of the gold extraterrestrial relics, with special permission from the Vatican.

Because this tunnel system and gold artifacts were so incredible and fantastic there was a great deal of interest in the reality of the claims, not just in Germany, but all over Europe and the World. Investigators and journalists flew to Ecuador to check out the story. Moricz then told the German magazine *Der Spiegel* that there had been no expedition into the caves and von Däniken's descriptions had come from "a long conversation." Moricz also said that the photos in the book had been "fiddled." He was referring to those that showed the cave walls to be seemingly square and man-made.

During the 1974 *Der Spiegel* interview, von Däniken asserted that he had indeed seen the library and the artifacts in the tunnels, but he had embellished some aspects of the story to make it more interesting. "In German we say a writer, if he is not writing pure science, is allowed to use some dramaturgische Effekte—some theatrical effects," he said. "And that's what I have done." Today he admits that he had never been inside Cueva de los Tayos with Moricz but felt that it was such a good story that he needed to embellish it a bit with the personal touch of having been inside the caves himself.

These caves do indeed exist and a multitude of strange stories are associated with them. The Father Crespi collection is real as well, and some of the artifacts may have come from the Tayos Caves. Juan Moricz is a very real person who continues to maintain that the Tayos Caves hold ancient artifacts and that parts of the caves have been artificially cut.

In 1976, a Scottish engineer named Stan Hall was driven by curiosity to go to Ecuador and check out Erich von Däniken's report of a metal library allegedly found in the caves by investigator Moricz in the mid-1960s. That year Hall organized a landmark expedition to the caves of the Tayos involving a dozen institutions, British Special Forces and astronaut professor Neil Armstrong as Honorary President and participant.

Although Hall and Armstrong did not find a metal library inside the caves, Hall was so fascinated by the caves and the story of the metal library that he pursued the subject for years, returning to Ecuador many times and cultivating special friendships that he reveals in his book *Tayos Gold*. In this book Hall writes about the caves, his explorations with Neil Armstrong, and his interest in the lost treasure of the Incas, lost explorers like Percy Fawcett and George Dyott, Atlantis, the Egyptian tablets of the Mormons, and other things. Hall's book, *Tayos Gold,* was published by Adventures Unlimited Press in 2007.

Other books have been published concerning the Tayos Caves and recently researcher Jim Veiera reported on his web pages that he had gone to

Ecuador with a small team to search for the Crespi Collection that had reportedly vanished shortly after Father Crespi's death in 1982. Veiera reports that his team determined that most of Father Crespi's collection is not missing but was purchased by the Central Bank of Ecuador and is currently stored in their museum vaults. He was able to view the artifacts at their vaults. Veiera also mentions the 4 minute and 52 second video that can be found on Youtube of Crespi showing the very artifacts that are pictured in this book to a British journalist. These artifacts have now disappeared. Says Veiera:

> A small subset of artifacts, which were photographed and filmed in the 1970s, consisting of gold carvings, hieroglyphs and Sumerian figures is genuinely missing and no one seems to have the answers as to where they are located and what their significance is.
>
> The missing artifacts consist not only of metallic (golden) tablets, but also clay and stone artifacts with unusual carvings, none of which were among the thousands of artifacts that we viewed in his collection held by the Central Bank of Ecuador. Some of the artifacts were accepted by Father Crespi as original and authentic, while others were fake, which he also knew and acknowledged. As a highly educated man—a scientist, educator, anthropologist, botanist, artist, explorer, cinematographer, humanitarian and musician—Father Crespi was in a good position to assess the authenticity of the artifacts.
>
> …we also managed to get in touch with an investigator who came to Ecuador around a decade ago to carry out his own search into the Father Crespi mystery. While he asked to remain anonymous, he did allow us to relay some information he obtained during his enquiries. Upon visiting the Central Bank Museum of Ecuador, where Crespi's artifacts are currently stored, he was told that the missing artifacts had been sold by the Church of Maria Auxiliadora, where Crespi carried out his charitable endeavors, to the Ecuadorian Military. He was also told that this information was confidential and not to be made public. We have been unable to verify the accuracy of this information, but it does add a new avenue to explore.

So, we now learn the possible fate of many of the artifacts that Erich speaks about in his sensational book, *The Gold of the Gods*. There is much to enjoy in this book: the mysterious artifacts of Ecuador, the strange tunnel systems, the massive basalt columns of Nan Madol—the eighth wonder of the world. Read on and enjoy.

—David Hatcher Childress,
Desert Redoubt, March 2020

1: *The Gold of the Gods*

To me this is the most incredible, fantastic story of the century. It could easily have come straight from the realms of Science Fiction if I had not seen and photographed the incredible truth in person.

What I saw was not the product of dreams or imagination, it was real and tangible.

A gigantic system of tunnels, thousands of miles in length and built by unknown constructors at some unknown date, lies hidden deep below the South American continent. Hundreds of miles of underground passages have already been explored and measured in Ecuador and Peru. That is only a beginning, yet the world knows nothing about it.

On 21 July, 1969, Juan Moricz, an Argentine subject, deposited a legal title-deed (fig. 1) signed by several witnesses with Dr Gustavo Falconi, a notary in Guayaquil. The deed sets out Moricz's claim to be the discoverer of the tunnels as far as the Republic of Ecuador and posterity are concerned. I had this document, which was written in Spanish, translated by a UN interpreter. I quote the most important parts of it at the beginning of this incredible story of mine:

'Juan Moricz, Argentine citizen by naturalisation, born in Hungary, Passport No 4361689 . . .

I have discovered objects of great cultural and historical value to mankind in the Province of Morona-Santiago, within the boundaries of the Republic of Ecuador.

The objects consist mainly of metal plaques inscribed

1

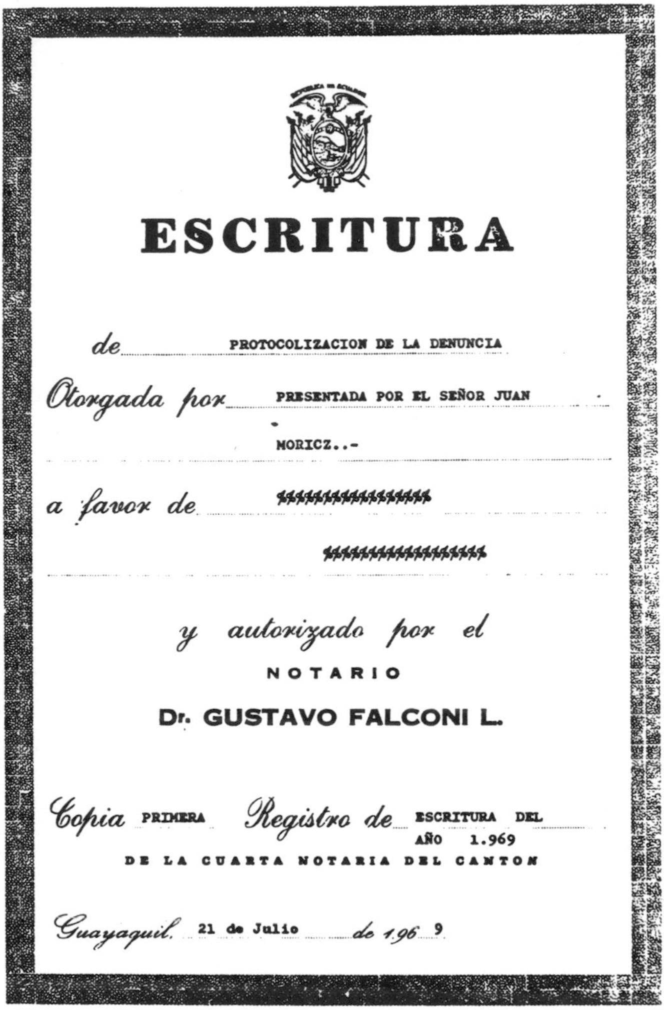

Fig. 1. With the issue of this notarial title-deed on 21 July, 1969, the caves beneath Ecuador became the property of Juan Moricz. Moricz put them under state control, which will smooth the way for future research.

with what is probably a résumé of the history of a lost civilisation, the very existence of which was unsuspected by mankind hitherto. The objects are distributed among various caves and are of many different kinds. I was able to make my discovery in fortunate circumstances . . . In my capacity as a scholar, I was carrying out research into the folklore and the ethnological and linguistic aspects of Ecuadorian tribes . . .

The objects I found are of the following kinds:

1. Stone and metal objects of different sizes and colours.

2. Metal plaques (leaves) engraved with signs and writing.

These form a veritable metal library which might contain a synopsis of the history of humanity, as well as an account of the origin of mankind on earth and information about a vanished civilisation.

The fact of my discovery has made me the legal owner of the metal plaques and other objects in accordance with Article 665 of the Civil Code.

However, as I am convinced that the objects, which were not found on my own land, are of incalculable cultural value, I refer to Article 666, according to which the treasure I discovered remains my personal property, but subject to State control.

I beg you, most excellent President of the Republic, to appoint a scientific commission to verify the contents of this document and assess the value of the finds . . .

I am prepared to show such a commission the exact geographical position and site of the entrance, as well as the objects I have discovered so far . . .'

Moricz stumbled on the underground passages in June, 1965, during his research work, in which he was ably assisted by Peruvian Indians who acted as skilful intermediaries between him and their tricky

fellow tribesmen. Being cautious by nature and sceptical as befitting a scholar, he kept silent for three years.
Not until he had covered many miles of underground
passages and found all kinds of remarkable objects did
he ask President Velasco Ibarra for an audience in the
spring of 1968. But the President of a country in which
nearly all his predecessors had been deposed by rebel-
lions before the expiry of their term of office, had no time
for this lone wolf with his incredible tale of discovery.
The palace flunkies found the obstinate archaeologist
very charming and assured him, after long delays, that
the President would be glad to receive him in a few
months' time, but Moricz was finally told he could not
have an audience until 1969. Disillusioned and embit-
tered he withdrew to his subterranean retreat.

I first met Juan Moricz on 4 March, 1972.

His lawyer, Dr Peña Matheus of Guayaquil, had been
trying to get in touch with him by telegram and telephone for two whole days. I had settled down in Dr
Peña's office with plenty to read, somewhat nervous, I
must admit, because according to all reports Moricz was
a very difficult man to approach and had a deep aversion
to anyone connected with the writing profession. Finally
one of the telegrams reached him. He telephoned me. He
knew my books! 'I don't mind talking to you,' he said.

On the night of 4 March he stood there, a wiry, deeply
tanned man in his mid-forties, with grey hair (fig. 2).
He is one of those men who has to be drawn out, because
he himself is anything but talkative. My vehement, insis-
tent questions amused him. Gradually he began to give a
factual and very expressive description of his tunnels.

'I can't believe it!' I cried.

'Nevertheless, it's just as he says,' said Dr Peña, 'I've
seen it all with my own eyes.'

Moricz invited me to visit the caves.

Fig. 2. Erich von Däniken with Juan Moricz, the discoverer of the caves, in front of a side-entrance to the mysterious underworld.

Moricz, Franz Seiner (my travelling companion) and I climbed into a Toyota jeep. During the twenty-four hour drive to the site we took turns at the wheel. Before we entered the caves, we took the precaution of having a good sleep. When the dawn sky announced the advent of a hot day, our adventure, the biggest in my life, began.

The entrance, cut in the rock and wide as a barn-door, is situated in the province of Morona-Santiago, in the triangle formed by Gualaquiza-San Antonio-Yaupi (fig. 3), a region inhabited by hostile Indians. Suddenly, from

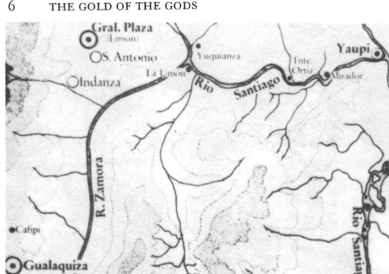

Fig. 3. The secret entrance to the hidden tunnel system, which is guarded by hostile Indians, is situated within the triangle formed by the three
towns Gualaquiza, San Antonio and Yaupi in the province of Morona-
Santiago.

one step to another, broad daylight changed to pitch
darkness. Birds fluttered past our heads. We felt the
draught they created and shrank back. We switched on
our torches and the lamps on our helmets, and there in
front of us was the gaping hole which led down into the
depths. We slid down a rope to the first platform 250 ft.
below the surface. From there we made two further des-
cents of 250 ft. Then our visit to the age-old underworld
of a strange unknown race really began. The passages
(fig. 4) all form perfect right angles. Sometimes they are
narrow, sometimes wide. The walls are smooth and often
seem to be polished. The ceilings are flat and at times
look as if they were covered with a kind of glaze.
Obviously these passages did not originate from natural
causes—they looked more like contemporary air-raid
shelters!

Fig. 4. Inside the artificial tunnel system, which is haunted by swarms of birds. In two places which I measured the droppings were 32–35 ins. deep. The ceilings are flat; the walls form right angles and are often covered with a kind of glaze.

As I was feeling and examining ceilings and walls, I burst out laughing and the sound echoed through the tunnels. Moricz shone his torch on my face:

'What's wrong? Have you gone crazy?'

'I'd like to see the archaeologist with the nerve to tell me that this work was done with hand-axes!'

My doubts about the existence of the underground tunnels vanished as if by magic and I felt tremendously happy. Moricz said that passages like those through which we were going extended for hundreds of miles under the soil of Ecuador and Peru.

'Now we turn off to the right,' called Moricz.

We stood at the entrance to a hall as big as the hangar of a Jumbo Jet. It could have been a distribution centre or a store-room, I thought. Galleries leading in different directions branched off it. When I tried to use my compass to find out where they led, it went on strike. I shook it, but the needle did not move. Moricz watched me:

'It's no use. There is radiation down here that makes it impossible to get a compass bearing. I don't know anything about the radiation, I have only observed it. It's really a job for physicists.'

On the threshold of a side passage a skeleton lay on the ground. It looked as if a doctor had carefully prepared it for an anatomy lesson, but in addition had sprayed it all over with gold dust. The bones gleamed in the light of our torches like solid gold.

Moricz told us to switch off our torches and follow him slowly. It was very quiet; all I could hear was our footsteps, our breathing and the whirr of the birds, to which we rapidly grew accustomed. The darkness was blacker than the darkest night.

'Switch on your torches,' shouted Moricz.

We were standing dumbfounded and amazed in the middle of a gigantic hall. Moricz, the proud discoverer, had prepared the effect as cleverly as the citizens of Brussels, who use the same trick when confronting foreign tourists with their Grand Place, perhaps the most beautiful square in the world.

This nameless hall into which the seventh passage leads is intimidatingly large, but very beautiful and nobly proportioned. We were told that the ground plan measures 153 by 164 yards. It went through my mind that these were almost the dimensions of the Pyramid of the Moon at Teotihuacan and that in both cases no one knows who the builders, the brilliant technicians, were.

There was a table in the middle of the room.

Was it really a table?

Presumably, for there were seven chairs along one side.

Were they chairs?

Apparently they were.

Stone chairs?

No, they did not have the same cold feeling as stone.

Were they made of wood?

Definitely not. Wood would never have lasted for thousands of years.

Were they made of metal?

I did not think so. They felt like some kind of plastic, but they were as hard and heavy as steel. There were animals behind the chairs: saurians, elephants, lions, crocodiles, jaguars, camels, bears, monkeys, bison, and wolves, with snails and crabs crawling about between them. Apparently they had been cast in moulds and there was no logical sequence about their arrangement. They were not in pairs, as is usual in pictures of Noah's Ark. They were not arranged by species, as zoologists prefer. Nor were they in the hierarchical order of natural evolution used by biologists. They simply stood there peacefully, as if the laws of nature did not apply.

The whole thing was like a fantastic zoo and what is more all the animals were made of solid gold.

Also in this hall was the most precious treasure of all, the metal library mentioned in the notarial title-deed, although I could never have guessed what it was really like from reading about it.

The library of metal plaques was opposite the zoo, to the left of the conference table. It consisted partly of actual plaques and partly of metal leaves only millimetres thick. Most of them measured about 3 ft. 2 ins. by 1 ft. 7 ins. After a long and critical examination, I still could not make out what material had been used in their manufacture. It must have been unusual, for the leaves stood upright without buckling, in spite of their size and thinness. They were placed next to each other like bound pages of giant folios. Each leaf had writing on it, stamped and printed regularly as if by a machine. So far Moricz has not managed to count the pages of his metal library, but I accept his estimate that there might be two or three thousand.

The characters on the metal plaques are unknown, but if only the appropriate scholars were told of the existence of this unique find *now* I am sure that they could be deciphered comparatively quickly in view of the wealth of possibilities for comparison.

No matter who the creator of this library was, nor when he lived, this great unknown was not only master of a technique for the 'mass-production' of metal folios in vast numbers—the proof is there—he also had written characters with which he wanted to convey important information to beings in a distant future. This metal library was created to outlast the ages, to remain legible for eternity.

Time will show whether our own age is seriously interested in discovering such fantastic, awe-inspiring secrets.

Is it prepared to decipher an age-old work even if it means bringing to light truths that might turn our neat but dubious world picture completely upside down?

Do not the high priests of all religions ultimately abhor revelations about prehistory that might replace *belief* in the creation by *knowledge* of the Creation?

Is man really prepared to admit that the history of his origin was entirely different from the one which is instilled into him in the form of a pious fairy story?

Are prehistorians really seeking the unvarnished truth without prejudice and partiality?

No one likes to fall off a skyscraper he has built himself.

The walls and passages of the tunnel system were bare. There were no paintings like those in the deep burial chambers in the Valley of the Kings near Luxor, no reliefs of the kind found in prehistoric caves at sites all over the world. Instead there were stone figures which we bumped into at every step.

Moricz owns a stone amulet $4\frac{1}{2}$ ins. high and $2\frac{1}{2}$ ins.

Fig. 5. An amulet dating to around 9000–4000 B.C. Moricz found it in the tunnels, which proves that they must be least equally old. A being stands on the terrestrial globe. How did Stone Age men know that the earth was round, a discovery that was not made until much later?

wide. The obverse (fig. 5) is engraved with a being with a hexagonal body and round head that might have been drawn by a child. The figure holds the moon in its right hand and the sun in its left hand. Admittedly, that is not particularly surprising, but—it stands with both feet firmly on the terrestrial globe! Surely that is a clear proof that even in times when the first primitive drawings were scratched on stone, a chosen few of our first ancestors already knew that we lived on a globe? The reverse shows a half moon and the radiant sun. Without any doubt, this stone amulet found in the tunnels seems to me to be a proof that they were already in existence in the Middle Palaeolithic (9000–4000 B.C.).

There is another engraving on a stone plaque (fig. 6),

Fig. 6. If this engraving by a prehistoric stonemason represents a dinosaur, there's something wrong! These animals lived 135,000,000 years ago.

$11\frac{1}{2}$ ins. high and 1 ft. $8\frac{1}{2}$ ins. wide, this time depicting an animal. I suspect that it is a representation of a dinosaur. This extinct prehistoric animal moved on land with the help of long hind legs as shown in the engraving. Even its gigantic size—dinosaurs were as much as 65 ft. long—

can still be sensed in the foreshortened squat version of the body, and the feet with three toes strengthen my suspicion. If my identification of this picture is correct, it will be most uncanny. This extinct reptile lived in the earth's Middle Ages during the Upper Cretaceous, i.e. 135,000,000 years ago, when the modern continents began to assume their present configuration. I am not going to speculate any further. I simply ask this question: what intelligent, thinking being ever saw a saurian?

In front of us lay the skeleton of a man, carved out of stone (fig. 7). I counted ten pairs of ribs, all anatomically accurate. Were there anatomists who dissected bodies for the prehistoric sculptor? As we know, Wilhelm Conrad Röntgen did not discover the new kind of rays he called X-rays until 1895!

In an office, I beg your pardon, a square stone room, Moricz showed me a dome (fig. 8). Figures with dark faces stood like guards around its circumference. They had hats on their heads and held spear-like objects in their hands, as if they were ready to defend themselves. Figures flew or floated through the air near the top of the dome. By the light of my torch I discovered a skeleton crouched behind the 'Romanesque' entrance to the dome. It did not shock me, but what did shock me was this model of a dome. Heinrich Schliemann discovered the first dome when he excavated Mycenae, a fortress and town in the north-east Peloponnese, from 1874–1876 B.C., and that dome was supposed to have been built by the Achaeans at the end of the fourteenth century B.C. I actually learnt at school that the Pantheon in Rome, built in Hadrian's reign between A.D. 120 and 125, was the first dome. But from now on I shall consider this piece of stonework as the oldest example of a dome.

A clown with a bulbous nose knelt on a stone plinth (fig. 9). The little fellow sported a helmet that covered his ears. Ear-phones like those on our telephones were

Fig. 7. A skeleton carved out of stone. Where did the sculptor get his knowledge from?

attached to the lobes of his ears. A ring in relief, with a diameter of 2 ins. and $\frac{2}{5}$ in. thick, was stuck to the front of the helmet. It was fitted with 15 holes, which seemed to be admirably adapted for fitting plugs into. A chain hung round his neck and it, too, had a ring with a

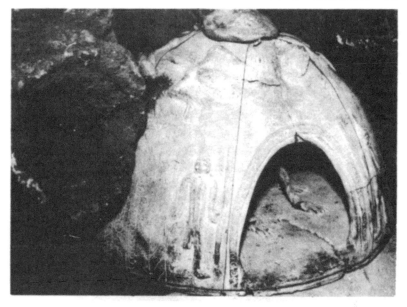

Fig. 8. Probably the very first dome ever built. What we were taught at school and what we read in books are no longer valid.

number of holes in it like those we use for dialling telephone numbers. Other remarkable features were the spacesuit accessories on the suit that the gnome wore, and the gloves, in which his fingers werc well protected against dangerous contacts.

I would not have paid any attention to a winged mother figure, between whose arms knelt a slit-eyed child in a crash-helmet, if I had not seen the identical figure (fig. 10), though in clay, during a visit to the American Museum in Madrid.

Whole books could and *will* be written about these tunnels and their treasures. Among many other things, they will mention the 6-ft. high stonemason's works, representing beings with three and seven heads; the triangular plaques, with writing on them as if schoolchildren had been making their first attempts at writing;

dice with geometrical figures on their six plane surfaces; the piece of soapstone, 3ft. 8 ins. long and 9¼ ins. wide, which is curved like a boomerang and covered with stars, etc.

Fig. 9. Clown, divinity or space traveller? The figure has such obviously technical accessories that he could easily have been one of a crew of cosmonauts. Mouthpiece, sockets on his helmet—what does it all mean?

No one knows who built the tunnels; no one knows the sculptors who left behind these strange ambiguous works. Only one thing seems clear to me. The tunnel builders were not the same men as the stonemasons; their stark practical passages were obviously not meant to be decorated. Perhaps they showed the underground vaults to a chosen group and the latter fashioned in stone things they had

seen and heard and stored the results in the depths.
So far the entrance to this underground treasure-trove

Fig. 10. The identical winged mother figure to the one in the caves in
Ecuador is on show in the American Museum in Madrid—but made of
clay!

of human history is known only to a few trustworthy
people and it is guarded by a wild Indian tribe. Indians
lurk unseen in the undergrowth and watch every movement made by strangers. Moricz has been accepted as a
friend by the chieftain of the cave guardians and three
members of the tribe who are occasionally in contact
with civilisation.

Once a year, at the beginning of spring, on 21 March,
the chieftain climbs down alone to the first platform in
the underworld to offer ritual prayers. Both his cheeks

Fig. 11. These markings are carved in the rock at the entrance to the tunnel. The chieftain of the tribe that guards the cave has identical markings on both cheeks. They are age-old Indian symbols.

bear the same signs as are marked in the rock at the entrance to the tunnels (fig. 11). To this day the tribe of tunnel guardians still make masks and carvings 'of the men with long noses' (gasmasks?) and they tell, as Moricz knows, of the heroic deeds of the 'flying beings' who once came from heaven. But the Indians will not go into the tunnels for love or money.

'No, no,' they said to Moricz. 'Spirits live down there.'

But it is a remarkable fact that Indian chiefs occasionally use gold to pay the debts they have incurred with the civilised world or present friends who have rendered their tribe a service with precious gold objects from their five-hundred-year-old past.

On several occasions Moricz had stopped me taking

photographs as we passed through the tunnels. He kept on making different excuses. Sometimes it was the radiation that would make the negatives unusable, sometimes it was the flash which might damage the metal library with its blinding light. At first I could not understand why, but after a few hours underground I began to sense the reason for Moricz's strange behaviour. You could not get rid of the feeling of being constantly watched, of destroying something magic, of unleashing a catastrophe. Would the entrances suddenly close? Would my flash ignite a synchronised laser beam? Would we never see the light of day again? Childish ideas for men engaged on serious investigation? Perhaps. But if you had experienced what it was like down there, you would understand these absurd ideas. Teams equipped with modern technical aids will have to work down there to see whether there are any dangers to be overcome or avoided.

When I first saw the pile of gold, I begged to be allowed to take just one photo. Once again I was refused. The lumps of gold had to be levered from the pile and that might make a noise and start stones falling from the roof like an avalanche. Moricz noticed my frustration and laughed.

'You'll be able to photograph plenty of gold later, but not in such vast quantities. Will that do?'

Today I know that the biggest gold treasure from the dark tunnels is not on show in South American museums. It lies in the back patio of the Church of Maria Auxiliadora at Cuenca in Ecuador, some 8,100 ft. above sea level.

Father Crespi (colour plate 4), the collector of the treasure, which is priceless just for its weight in gold, has been living in Cuenca for forty-five years. He is accepted as a trustworthy friend of the Indians, who during past decades fetched the most valuable gold and silver objects from their hiding-places piece by piece and gave them to him, and still do so today.

I had been warned beforehand that the good Father was fond of pulling his visitors' legs. I soon had a taste of this. In all seriousness he showed me an object that was obviously the lower part of a flat-iron. 'Look,' he said, 'that proves that the Inca rulers had their trousers pressed even in those days!' We laughed and Father Crespi led us through his treasure chambers. Room I houses stonemason's work; room II contains Inca artefacts of gold, silver, copper and brass, while room III holds the gold treasure, which he very seldom shows anyone, and then unwillingly. Cuenca has a 'Gold Museum' of its own, but it cannot compare with Father Crespi's.

So if from now on I frequently mention gold and pure gold at that, I am simply repeating my own and Father Crespi's conviction; it is indeed pure gold that has now been brought to the notice of an incredulous and astonished world by my camera.

The showpiece was a stele (colour plate 11), $20\frac{1}{2}$ ins. high, $5\frac{1}{2}$ ins. wide and $1\frac{1}{2}$ ins. thick. 56 different characters are 'stamped' on its 56 squares. I had seen absolutely identical characters on the leaves in the metal library in the Great Hall! Whoever made this gold stele used a code (an alphabet?) with 56 letters or symbols arranged to form writing. What makes this all the more remarkable is the fact that hitherto it has always been claimed that the South American cultures (Mayas, Incas, etc.) possessed no alphabetical writing or script with alphabetical characteristics.

'Have you seen this lady?' asked Moricz.

She was $12\frac{1}{2}$ ins. high and naturally of solid gold. Her head was formed of two triangles, whose planes seemed to have wings welded to them. Coiled cables emerged from her ears; they were obviously not jewellery, for the lady's earrings were clipped to her ear lobes.

She had healthy, if triangular proportions, with well-formed breasts and stood with legs apart. The fact that she had no arms did not mar her beauty. She wore long elegant trousers. A sphere floated above her head and I felt that the stars on either side referred to her origin. A star from a past age? A maiden from the stars?

Next came a gold discus, $8\frac{1}{2}$ ins. in diameter (colour plate 2). It cannot have been a shield, as the archaeologists would catalogue it. For one thing it is too heavy, for another it has never had a hand-hold on its smooth reverse side. I believe that this discus, too, was intended to transmit information. It exhibits two stylised, but incredibly accurate spermatozoa, two laughing suns, the sickle of a waning moon, a large star and two stylised triangular men's faces. In the middle are small raised circles, arranged to give the beholder visual pleasure, but apparently intended to produce a different and more serious effect. Father Crespi put a heavy gold plaque in front of the camera.

'Here is something special for you, my young friend. This piece dates to the period before the Flood.'

Three creatures, holding a tall tablet with some signs on it, stared at me. The pairs of eyes looked as if they were peering from behind goggles. The upper left-hand monster pointed to a sphere, the right-hand one was clad from head to foot in an overall, which was fastened at the sides, and proudly wore a three-cornered star on his head. Above the tablet with signs floated two winged spheres. What were the monsters holding? Some kind of Morse code, dots, dashes, SOS's? A switchboard for electric contacts? Anything is possible, but I suspect technical analogies rather than letters on this tablet. And according to the Father, who has been given special Vatican permission to carry out his archaeological research, it does date to the period before the Flood.

Take my word for it, when you catch sight of the treasures in the back patio of Maria Auxiliadora, you have to be very strong-willed not to get 'gold-drunk'. But it was not the large amounts of gold that impressed me, it was the representation of stars, moons, suns and snakes that gleamed on hundreds of metal plaques—nearly all of them unequivocal symbols of space travel.

I picked some exceptionally photogenic examples of such pictures out of what is presumably the lost heritage of the Incas, who were very familiar with the snake sign and used it decoratively in representations of their ruler, the 'Son of the Sun'. Here they are:

A gold relief with a pyramid (colour plate 5). The steep sides are bordered by *snakes*. There are two suns, two astronaut-like monsters, two deer-like animals and some circles with dots in them. Do the circles indicate the number of space travellers buried inside the pyramid?

Another gold plaque with a pyramid (colour plate 3). Two jaguars, symbols of strength, have their paws on the sides. There are obvious signs of writing at the foot of the pyramid. To the right and left we see elephants, which lived in South America about 12,000 years ago before any civilisations or cultures are supposed to have existed. And the *snakes* are at last where they ought to be, in the sky.

No one can deny that snakes and dragons have a special place in all myths about the creation. Even a scientist such as Dr Irene Sänger-Bredt, who is an engineer in the aircraft and space industries, puts the following question in her book *Ungelöste Rätsel der Schöpfung (Unsolved Puzzles of the Creation):*

'Why does the dragon motif play such an important part in the figurative representations and

myths of the ancient Chinese, Indians, Babylon-
ians, Egyptians, Jews, Germans and Mayas?'

In her answer, Dr Sänger-Bredt thinks it probable that
snake and dragon symbols must have some connection
with the creation and the universe.

In his book *The Masters of the World*, Robert Charroux
quotes ancient texts to show that gleaming snakes which
floated in the air have occurred everywhere, that the
Phoenicians and Egyptians raised snakes and dragons to
the godhead, and that the snake belonged to the element
of fire, because in it *there is a speed which nothing can exceed,
because of its breath*. Charroux quotes Areios of Heracleo-
polis literally: 'The first and highest divinity is the snake
with the sparrow-hawk head; when it opens its eyes, it
fills the whole of the newly created world with light;
when it shuts them, the darkness spreads over everything.'

The historian Sanchuniaton, who lived in Beirut *circa*
1250 B.C., is reputed to have recorded the mythology and
history of the Phoenicians. Charroux quotes this passage
from him:

> 'The snake has a speed which nothing can exceed,
> because of its breath. It can impart any speed it likes
> to the spirals it describes as it moves . . . Its energy is
> exceptional . . . With its brilliance it has illuminated
> everything.'

These are not descriptions of the sort of snakes that
intelligent human beings saw crawling about on the
ground.

But why have snakes so persistently made their home
in all the creation stories and myths?

For once, I shall obey the call of the scholars, according to whom our primaeval ancestors can only be

understood in terms of their own mental level at the
time when they lived, and use simple depth psychology.

If our ancestors saw a large unusual bird, they
described what they had actually seen, as the concept for
it was included in their limited vocabulary. But how
could they have described a phenomenon in the firmament seen for the first time for which words and concepts
were lacking? Probably the alien cosmonauts were not
over-particular about casualties during their first landing
on our planet. Perhaps spectators were hit and scorched
by the red-hot trail of a jet during the landing or destroyed by the thrust of a rocket on the return launching.
There was absolutely no technical vocabulary for an eye-
witness account of this terrifying yet grandiose event.
The unknown gleaming (metal) thing that landed or
took off, snorting, smelling and kicking up a din was
obviously not a bird. So they described what they had
seen—using current ideas—as a thing 'like a dragon' or
'like a great gleaming bird', or, because it was so far
beyond their comprehension, as 'a feathered fire-
breathing serpent'. Horrified by what they had experienced, fathers told their sons and they told their grand-
sons for centuries and millennia about the terrifying
apparition of the dragon or snake. With the passage of
time the eye-witness account using a make-shift vocabulary gradually became vaguer. Sometimes the fire-
breathing dragon would loom largest, sometimes the
flying snake, until they assumed their predominant position in mythology.

There are countless snakes on the gold plaques in the
tunnels underneath Ecuador and Peru, and on Father
Crespi's treasures: snakes crawling up pyramids, striving
for the summits, flying in the heavens with a trail of fire
or lying on the heads of the gods. But neither here nor
elsewhere do we see a single snake doing the things men
have always seen them do—wriggling through the grass,

hanging from a tree, swallowing a mouse or writhing about in the mud with other snakes.

Everywhere dragons and even more so snakes stand as symbols for phenomena from the cosmos.

What do the archaeologists say about all this?

The snake was a symbol of immortality. Why? Because our observant ancestors had noticed that the reptile shed its skin and constantly emerged from it renewed. Surely our ancestral students of behaviour observed that in the end the snake died just the same?

The snake was an expression of agility and manoeuvrability. Would not birds or butterflies have been better models than this miserable creature crawling on the ground?

The snake was an emblem of fertility and was honoured as such by primitive peoples—all of whom were afraid of snakes. A strange stimulus to the production of offspring.

Forest dwellers were afraid of the snake and so they chose it as a god. Lions, bears or jaguars are much more dangerous—snakes only seize animals that they want to eat, they do not attack indiscriminately.

Moses gets nearer to the truth (Genesis 1, 3). For him the snake is the messenger of disaster, much as in the North Germanic Midgard of early times, that 'farm' between heaven and earth, the snake coils round the property as the personification of danger and destructive power.

Prehistoric evidence shows:

that snakes and dragons are connected with the creation of men;

that snakes and dragons are connected with the stars;

that snakes can fly;

that snakes have an unpleasant fiery breath.

So far there has been no profound investigation of the

origin of snakes in myths and legends in archaeological and ethnological literature. Experts could fill this gap. I gladly place my archives at their disposal.

Father Crespi has partially stacked his gold plaques by motifs, for example those with pictures of pyramids. I took a close look at more than 40 and some of them are reproduced in this book. *All* the pyramid engravings have four things in common:

a sun, but more frequently several suns, is depicted above the pyramid;

snakes are always flying next to or over the pyramid;

animals of various kinds are always present;

two concentric circles in varying numbers, but always of the same size, are engraved near the pyramids. I counted between 9 and 78.

These concentric circles, actually a large dot inside a circle, are not only found here at Cuenca, but in all kinds of prehistoric cave paintings and reliefs. Until now these dotted circles were and still are interpreted as solar symbols. I have my doubts about this. The sun (with laughing face or a corona of rays) always has a place reserved for it in addition; in fact, frequently several suns are shining. If the suns are depicted so unmistakably, we ought to ask ourselves what the circles have to tell us. Do they indicate the numbers of astronauts observed? When they occur near the pyramid, are they an indication of the number of alien gods buried inside them? Or do they mark the sequence of explosions observed? I believe that the dotted circles are purely and simply a form of reckoning. What I mean cannot be more graphically depicted than in the cave painting which was discovered in the Kimberley Ranges, Australia (fig. 12). The god's 'halo' symbolises the sun, but 62 circles are painted next to the figure. Are these simply meant to be small suns? There are all kinds of possible questions and I find any answer more likely than the claim that the dotted circles, even when they are next to obvious pictures of the sun, represent yet more solar symbols. Our prehistoric message transmitters did not make things all that easy for us.

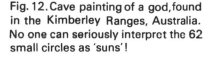

Fig. 12. Cave painting of a god, found in the Kimberley Ranges, Australia. No one can seriously interpret the 62 small circles as 'suns'!

In addition animals are always present. I cannot resist one more taunt. At the foot of the pyramid made with great accuracy of neat blocks stand two delightful elephants. That's nice.

Archaeologists have dug up elephants' bones in North America and Mexico, but they were dated to before 12,000 B.C. But elephants had completely disappeared from the scene in South America in the age of the Incas, whose culture, it is established, began around A.D. 1200. So we must make a choice: either the Incas had received visitors from Africa who drew elephants next to the pyramids for them or these gold plaques are more than 14,000 years old (12,000 plus 2000). The only answer is either/or.

I think that the pyramids stamped in gold from Father Crespi's treasure help to eliminate an academic error. Until now scholars have asserted that both the pyramids in South America and the Mayan pyramids in Central America originated without any connection with the Egyptian pyramids. In Egypt the colossal structures were burial places, in the other hemisphere simply grandiose edifices on the upper platforms of which temples were built. The gold plaques do not exhibit a single flattened surface at the summit with a temple on it! They have *the same* pyramidal shapes as those in Egypt. Who copied from whom? Who were the first to build pyramids, the Incas or the Egyptians? They cannot be posthumous forgeries. Firstly forgers would have needed more gold than there is in Fort Knox, secondly, they would have needed to employ a whole corps of artists with a far-reaching knowledge of the ancient peoples and their cultures, and thirdly it would have been necessary to continue making the grandiose forgeries right through the Inca period, whenever that was.

I should like to know what tricks scholars will use to displace this fabulous gold treasure of inestimable archaeological and historical value, which is described here for the first time, from the period into which it does not seem to fit. Could it be that *all* pyramids *everywhere* in the world had the same master-builders?

Characters can often be made out on the illustrated gold objects from Cuenca. Are they older than all previously known forms of writing?

Cuneiform writing in Phoenicia and hieroglyphics in Egypt are supposed to have originated *circa* 2000 B.C. from a mixture of Egyptian and Babylonian influences.

Circa 1700 B.C. the pre-Israelite population of Palestine is supposed to have created a simplified syllabic script with

Phönizisch 12. bis 10. Jh. v. Chr.

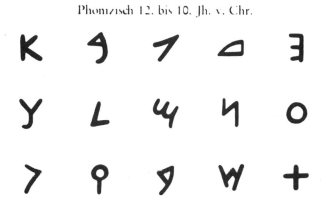

Fig. 13. Phoenician alphabet, 12th–10th century B.C. All the alphabets in the world originated from the Phoenician alphabet with its 22 signs. At least that was the accepted theory until now.

about 100 signs, composed of a mixture of both the foregoing kinds of writing. The Phoenician alphabet with 22 signs (fig. 13) developed from this shortly before 1500 B.C. With the addition or transformation of signs all the alphabets in the world derive from the Phoenician one. About 1000 B.C. the Greeks adopted two variations of the Phoenician alphabet; they left out some expendable consonantal signs and used them to represent vowels, and that is how the first phonetic script in the world originated.

For generations all the scholars specialising in this field have claimed that neither the pre-Inca peoples nor the Incas themselves had an alphabetical script. They marvelled at the Indians' civilised achievements, their road-building and water-supply systems, the accurate calendar, the Nazca culture, the buildings at Cuzco, their highly developed agriculture, an (oral) postal service that worked and many other things. The one thing they would not credit them with was writing or an alphabet.

Professor Thomas Barthel, Director of the Folklore Institute of Tübingen University, told the 39th International Congress of American Studies at Lima that he had succeeded in establishing 400 signs of an Inca writing. He could interpret the meaning of 50 of them and read 24. It was not an alphabetical script. Peruvian and German scholars spoke of 'attractive patterns and ornaments', which they thought were akin to writing.

In January 1972, a veritable bomb exploded on the Congress for Andean Archaeology at Lima. The Peruvian ethnologist Dr Victoria de la Jara backed up ten years of research work with proof that the Incas really did have a script. She said that the geometrical patterns (squares, right-angles, lozenges, dots, dashes, etc.) on Inca pottery and urns were in fact characters with a content ranging from the simple to the highly complicated. They related factual historical events, they recounted myths and proved that even then some of the Incas practised the noble but ill-paid art of poetry. Groups of elements formed a grammar based on complementary colours. When Dr de la Jara finished her lecture, there was thunderous applause from her fellow scholars.

What will the ethnologists say when they begin to rack their brains over the writing on the gold plaques at Cuenca? I know perfectly well that there will be no thunderous applause for me, but I still say that the characters on these gold plaques found deep under the earth will prove to be the oldest writing in the world! And that wise messengers from the gods inscribed technical data and advice for future generations on them!

I have seen three prehistoric model aircraft of ultra-modern design!

Anyone who travels to Colombia can see the first one (fig. 14) on show in the State Bank at Bogota. The

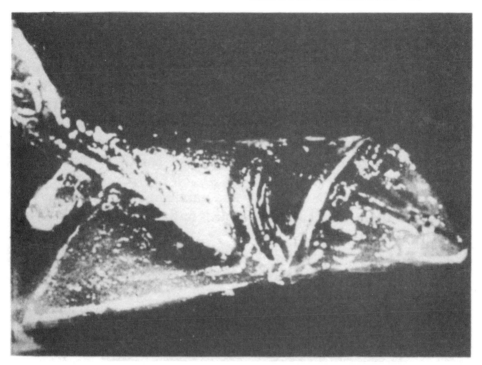

Fig. 14. This gold model of a Concorde is in the State Bank, Bogota. It can't be incorporated into any fish or bird cult. There weren't any!

second is naturally owned by Father Crespi and the third still lies 780 ft. below ground in Juan Moricz's tunnels.

For centuries archaeologists have catalogued the model at Bogota as a decorative religious artefact. I'm sorry for the archaeologists, but that simply won't do. Aviation experts have seen the object and tried it out in a wind tunnel. They believe it is a model aircraft. Dr Arthur Poyslee of the Aeronautical Institute, New York, says:

'The possibility that the artefact is meant to represent a fish or a bird is very slight. Not only because this gold model was found deep in the interior of Colombia and artists would never have seen a salt-water fish, but also because one cannot imagine a bird with such geometrical wings and high vertical fins.'

The front part is as clumsy as that of the heaviest US B52. The pilot's cockpit lies directly behind the streamlined nose, protected by a windscreen. The aircraft's rear, heavy with the propulsion unit it contains, rests in aerodynamic symmetry on two rounded-off wings. (The model at Bogota has two delta wings like the Concorde and terminates, like it, in a sharply pointed nose.) Two stabilising fins and the upright tail complete the Inca model aircraft (fig.15).

Who could be so dreary and unimaginative as to interpret these model aircraft as birds or flying fish?

Fig. 15. The Aeronautical Institute, New York, made these technical drawings after accurate testing in a wind tunnel.

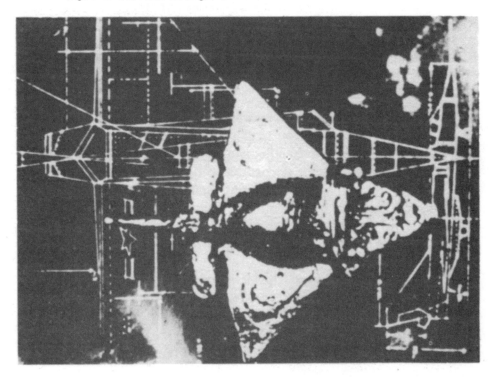

In all ages gold was a rare and consequently precious metal; it was found in temples and royal palaces. If an object was cast in gold, it was because it had great value *per se* and also because it was to be preserved for an indefinite period of time. Hence it was made of a material that did not rust or corrode. Anyway, there was no fish or bird cult to which these models could be attributed.

There is a massive gold sphere (coloured plate 1), with a broad flange round it, in the cosmological treasury at Maria Auxiliadora. To anticipate fatuous objections, it is not a sculptural representation of a hat with a brim. Hats have hollow spaces for even the most stupid heads to fit

The constructors modified the archaeologists' 'religious artefact' with these drawings!

into.

In *Gods from Outer Space*, I showed—without contradiction—why I consider that the sphere is the ideal shape for spaceships or space-stations. Spherical bodies rotate in space, thus creating an artificial gravity for the crew in the cabins placed at the sphere's circumference. (Gravity is necessary for the metabolism of the organs on lengthy journeys.) The gold sphere once again supports my contention that the sphere was the shape used for celestial vehicles in distant ages.

In addition to serving as a docking ramp for supply ships, the broad flange may also have been divided into cells to store solar energy. The technical possibilities, we can imagine, are endless.

At all events, I should like to *know* how the matrix (fig.

16) of this gold sphere came to be in Turkey, 7,500 miles
from Ecuador! This find, carved out of stone, is on show
in the Turkish Museum, Istanbul. It is the negative of
the gold sphere in Father Crespi's treasure: the same
sphere, the same notched pattern on the encircling rim.
The card under the stone matrix in the first storey of the
Museum at Istanbul says 'Unclassifiable'. As long as
science refuses to accept the idea that flying machines
could cross the oceans and cover the vast distances between the continents as early as prehistoric times, its
rigid prejudice will find certain puzzles insoluble.

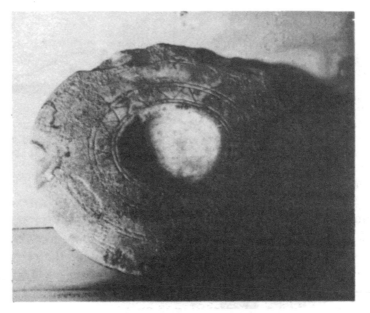

Fig. 16. The matrix, the negative, of the golden space sphere from
Cuenca is on show in the Turkish Museum at Istanbul!

One cannot say that scholars have no imagination, but
the fact remains that they insist on new discoveries fitting
into accepted patterns.

At Cuenca I photographed a gold object, some 20 ins.
high, representing a figure of normal human dimensions

(colour plate 6). An abnormal feature is that he has only four fingers on each hand and four toes on each foot. However, we also find representations of the gods with some of their limbs missing among the ancient Indians, the Maoris, the Etruscans and other peoples.

Yet I read in a serious scientific publication how simple the solution of this mystery is. Toes and fingers were a kind of adding machine. If the artist wanted to express the number '19', he left out one finger or one toe. Pursuing this scholarly fantasy, the number '16' was represented as a being with four plus four toes and four plus four fingers = 16! This ingenuous way of counting seems to me to be unworthy of a people who built roads and fortresses and cities.

Why, by the gods of all the stars, did the intelligent Incas have to draw or sculpt a whole man with hands and feet to express the number 4? Deadly serious science gets entangled in the net of its own fantasy. To be sure it admits that the Incas *could* count, but it does not credit them with being able to represent '4' by four dots or four dashes. So they had to lop off fingers and toes. *O sancta simplicitas!*

As for the figure that is minus two fingers and two toes, the explanation as a childish method of counting is unconvincing, for according to Father Crespi, it is a representation of the 'Star God'. In his right arm the smiling sun god clasps an animal combination of hippopotamus, parrot and snake, in his left, a staff with his emblem, the laughing sun at the top and a decorative snake's head at the bottom. Star-like points surround the god's happy face and they can be seen, too, on his two colleagues from caves in the Australian bush, the two 'creators' (fig. 17). They wear overalls with broad straps around the chest.

At some time in the future, probably after the metal library has been deciphered, it will transpire that figures

with anatomically inaccurate limbs are really pictorial
representations of traditional oral descriptions of phenomena from the cosmos that were different.

The masterpiece of the Inca's Dürer, Degas or Picasso,
is a gold plaque measuring 38½ ins. by 19 ins. by 1 in. No
matter how long one studies it, one keeps on making new
discoveries. I noted down what I found: a star, a being
with a fat paunch and a snake's tail, a rat-like animal, a
man in a coat of mail and a helmet, a man with a triangular head from which rays emanate, two faces, a wheel
with a face peeping out of it, birds, snakes, bald and
hairy heads, a face that grows out of another one, a snake
with a face, two concentric circles with a face inside. A
veritable riot! Paired together amid all the disorder are

Fig. 17. These funny mythical figures, primaeval inhabitants of Australia,
known as the 'two creators', have the same star-like points as the 'Star God',
which is 'sold' to us as a calculating machine.

two strong gold 'hinges', which bring into prominence a face above a falling bomb! (Colour plate 7.)

What was the artist trying to convey?

Was he a predecessor of Hieronymus Bosch?

Has he perpetuated the moment of the annihilation of earthly chaos by the Star God?

The minute fraction of the treasure from the patio of the Church of Maria Auxiliadora at Cuenca that I have illustrated here is a still more minute fraction of the precious objects which rest undisturbed in Juan Moricz's tunnels, an orgy of human history in gold.

What were the Incas' gold objects for, what was their purpose? Are they simply expensive primitive toys?

Or are they really messages from a very early age that we cannot decipher?

Professor Miloslav Stingl is the leading South American scholar in the Iron Curtain countries; he graduated in the ancient civilisations of America. Today he is a member of the Academy of Sciences at Prague and author of archaeological and ethnological books. *In versunkenen Mayastädten* (1971), for example, is highly acclaimed. Professor Stingl, who was a guest in my house, saw the photographs I had taken at Cuenca.

'If these pictures are genuine, and everything indicates that they are, because no one makes forgeries in gold, at any rate not on such a large scale, this is the biggest archaeological sensation since the discovery of Troy. Years ago I myself supported the view that the Incas had no writing in the alphabetical sense of the word. And now I'm faced with Inca writing! It must be very, very ancient, because one can recognise the transition from ideograms to writing.'

'What do you make of the engravings? How do you fit them into the existing system?'

'To be able to give a precise scientific verdict I should

have to subject each plaque to a detailed and lengthy examination, and compare each one with material already available. For the moment I can only say that I am dumbfounded. The sun was often part of the scenery in known Inca engravings, but man was never equated with the sun, as I see time and again in these photographs. There are representations of men with sun's rays round their heads and there are men depicted with star points coming from them. The symbol of "holy power" has always been the head. But in these pictures the head is simultaneously sun or star. That points to new direct connections.'

'How would you interpret the bomb on the plaque?'

The famous scholar took out a magnifying-glass and examined the photograph in silence for a long time.

'No interpretation is possible; all this is absolutely new. Explained in totemistic terms, I would say the radiant figures with the stars above and the snake symbols below indicate a connection between heaven and earth. And that means that the stellar beings and suns had a relationship with the inhabitants of the earth.'

'What else?'

'I cannot say any more. Of course, the solar wheel is well known, but here it is not clear whether it *is* a solar wheel, for there is a face inside it, which is quite contradictory. At all events, all the figures, birds, snakes, helmeted figures and everything else that can be seen on the plaque seem to originate from a dream world, from a mythology.'

'A mythology that is daily acquiring a more tangible and realistic background!'

The professor laughed: 'I have to admit that you have arguments in your jigsaw puzzle that disconcert even an old fox like me and give me cause for reflection.'

Who is going to study the tunnels and treasures underneath Ecuador, who is going to bring this sensational archaeological discovery into the searching light of scientific examination? There does not seem to be anyone available as rich and enthusiastic as Heinrich Schliemann, who excavated Troy and Mycenae. When Moricz discovered the tunnels he was as poor as a church mouse. Since then he has discovered iron and silver mines and leased them to metal firms to exploit. He has become comparatively rich, but he lives extremely simply and uses all his wealth for his research work. But Juan Moricz is not rich enough to engage expert assistance and continue his work on the extended scale that is essential. He knows perfectly well that he could immediately get the help of speculators, Wild West type gold-diggers; he would only have to show them a fraction of the alluring gold treasures in the tunnels below Ecuador. He does not want that kind of assistance. It would degenerate into plundering and would not benefit mankind. That is why it is difficult to organise a disinterested expedition that would be exclusively devoted to research. Even in 1969 when Moricz invited guests to visit the site, he had the group accompanied by armed guards. Moricz and Peña said that the further the group penetrated into the labyrinth, the tenser and more febrile grew the atmosphere, until finally the guests were afraid of the guards, who had caught gold fever. They all had to turn back.

Why does Ecuador do nothing to encourage a scientific expedition that would bring fame to the country?

Ecuador, with its five million inhabitants, is one of the poorest countries in South America. The plantations of cocoa, bananas, tobacco, rice and sugar-cane do not bring in enough foreign exchange for the purchase of modern technical equipment. Indian agriculture on the plateaux produces potatoes and corn, and there is some sheep and lama breeding. The wild rubber obtained from the eastern forests is no longer in demand. Perhaps government-aided exploitation of mineral wealth (gold, silver, copper, lead and manganese) may bring in some income in the years to come, as may the petroleum found offshore. But even then all the surplus will be used in the first place to alleviate the wretched poverty; as yet the government shows no interest in projects that do not directly help to overcome the problem of hunger.

Juan Moricz estimates that inspection of the tunnel system alone, without detailed research, would cost more than one million Swiss francs. An electricity station would have to be set up, security measures would have to be taken and some form of mining machinery would be necessary.

My knowledge of this buried treasure, which has so much to tell us about human history, induces me to repeat the challenge I issued in *Gods from Outer Space* in 1968:

> 'A Utopian archaeological year is due! During this year archaeologists, physicists, chemists, geologists, metallurgists and all the allied branches of these disciplines would concentrate on one question: did our ancestors receive visits from outer space?'

Fig. 18. Lawyer Peña tells every serious research worker how to get in touch with Juan Moricz! The tunnels under Ecuador need detailed investigation!

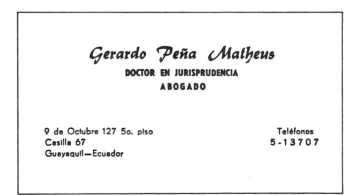

Gerardo Peña Matheus

DOCTOR EN JURISPRUDENCIA
ABOGADO

9 de Octubre 127 5o. piso
Casilla 67
Guayaquil—Ecuador

Teléfonos
5-13707

So that no individual or institution can say that it is out of the question to go in search of nebulous mysterious caves, I print here lawyer Peña's visiting-card. He will gladly put any serious investigator in touch with Juan Moricz. (Fig. 18.)

Nearby, in the Peruvian Andes, Francisco Pizarro (1478–1541) discovered cave entrances closed with slabs of rock on Huascaran, the mountain of the Incas, 22,203 ft. above sea-level. The Spaniards suspected that there were store-rooms behind them.

Speleologists did not remember these caves until 1971, when an expedition was organised. The periodical *Bild der Wissenschaft* gave an account of the expedition which descended in the neighbourhood of the Peruvian village of Otuzco equipped with all the latest technical equipment (winches, electric cables, miner's lamps and hydrogen bottles). 200 ft. below the earth the scientists made a staggering discovery. At the far end of caves which had several storeys they suddenly found themselves confronted with water-tight doors made of gigantic slabs of rock. In spite of their tremendous weight, four men were able to push the doors open. They pivoted on stone balls in a bed formed by dripping water.

Bild der Wissenschaften reported as follows:

'Vast tunnels, which would leave even modern underground constructors green with envy, began behind the "six doors". These tunnels lead straight towards the coast, at times with a slope of 14 per cent. The floor is covered with stone slabs that have been pitted and grooved to make them slip-proof. If it is an adventure even today to penetrate these 55 to 65 mile-long transport tunnels in the direction of the coast and finally reach a spot 80 ft. below sea level, imagine the difficulties that must have been involved in the fourteenth and fifteenth centuries in transporting goods

deep under the Andes to save them from the grasp of
Pizarro and the Spanish Viceroy. The Great Ocean
lurks at the end of the underground passages of 'Guanape', so called after the island that lies off the coast of
Peru here, because it is assumed that these passages
once led under the sea to this island. After the passages have gone uphill and downhill several times in
pitch darkness, a murmur and the strangely hollow
sounding noise of surf is heard. In the light of the
searchlight the next downhill slope ends on the edge of
a pitch black flood which is identified as seawater. The
present-day coast also begins here underground. Was
this not the case in former times?'

Scholars think that a search on the island of Guanape
would be pointless, because there is nothing there to
indicate that a passage from the mainland ever emerged
on to it. 'No one knows where these subterranean roads
of the Incas and their ancestors end or whether they lead
the way to the bursting treasuries of worlds that vanished
long ago.'
Francisco Pizarro and his rapacious followers had
already suspected that gold treasures existed in impenetrable Inca hiding places. In 1532 the noble Spaniard
promised the Inca ruler Atahualpa his life and freedom if
he filled two-thirds of a room measuring 23 by 16 by 10
ft. with gold. Atahualpa believed the word of the ambassador of Her Christian Majesty Juana the Mad
(1479–1555). Day after day the Incas fetched gold until
the room was filled to the required height. Then Pizarro
broke his word and had Atahualpa executed (1533).
In the same year the Spanish Viceroy elevated the Inca
Manco Capac to the rank of shadow king. (He, too, was
murdered by the Christian conquerors in 1544.) His
death saw the end of the Inca dynasty, which had
entered history with its legendary founder of the same

name. According to the historians, 13 'Sons of the Sun' are supposed to have ruled the Inca kingdom between the first and the last Manco Capac. If we date its historically established beginning to around A.D. 1200 and its end to 1544, the year when the last sun king died, then this mighty empire that stretched from Chile to Ecuador, from the Andes north of Quito to Valparaiso in the south, must have been built up in barely 350 years. During this period, the first pre-Columbian empire in South America must have been welded together. For the conquered territories and peoples were not considered as occupation zones, but were integrated into the prevailing constitution. Progressive achievements in agriculture were passed on by trained officials, as were the smoothly functioning rules of a communal economic order.

Did the Incas equip a network of 2,500 miles of well-built roads with rest-houses during the same span of time? Did they simultaneously build cities such as Cuzco, Tiahuanaco, Macchu Picchu, and the cyclopean fortresses of Oliantaytambo and Sacsahuamán? Did they also lay down water mains and work silver, tin and copper mines, whose products they alloyed to make bronze? And did they develop the goldsmith's art, weave the finest cloth and make pottery with noble shapes 'on the side', as it were? I hardly dare speak of the high culture which they nurtured in addition during this limited 350 year period. But if, it was not the Incas, but their ancestors who should be credited with these wonderful achievements, surely the culture and tool technology of the pre-Inca peoples must have been higher than the Incas who came after them.

No, the chronology cannot be blindly pasted together like that, because there are so many indications to turn the arbitrary (re-)construction upside down.

I assert that the tunnel system existed thousands of years before the Inca kingdom came into being. (How and with what tools are the Incas supposed to have built hundreds of miles of passages deep under the earth? The Channel tunnel has been planned by the engineers of our highly technological century for fifty years and they still have not decided which method should be used to build this comparatively minor tunnel.)

I assert that the age-old tunnel systems were known to the Inca ruling classes. (After Atahualpa's murder, the last Manco Capac ordered the gold treasures scattered throughout the kingdom to be collected in the Temple of the Sun and deposited in the *existing caves, which were known to him*, to keep them safe from the white invaders.)

I assert that the gold treasures under Ecuador and Peru come from a period long before the rise of the Inca kingdom and its culture. About 1570 the Spanish chronicler Pater Cristobal de Molina tried to fathom the motives behind the Incas' tunnel building. In his book *Ritos y Fabulos de los Incas*, published in 1572, Molina tells us that the original father of mankind withdrew into a cave after he had done his work, i.e. after the creation was completed. But this secret retreat became the birthplace of many peoples who had appeared out of an 'endless night'. Molina related that these caves were also used for generations as treasuries for hiding the peoples' wealth whenever they were oppressed. Absolute secrecy in the circles who knew about the caves was an iron law, non-compliance with which was punishable by death. (How potent this law still is today I was able to experience on my journey through Ecuador in the year of grace 1972.)

Let the Vatican grail guardian Father Crespi of Cuenca be the key witness to the pre-Christian origin of the gold treasures. He said to me:

'Everything that the Indians brought me from the tunnels dates to before Christ. Most of the gold symbols and pre-historic representations are older than the Flood.'

Three kinds of treasure await excavation in the tunnels and halls under Ecuador and Peru:

1. The inexhaustible legacy of the builders of the actual tunnels;

2. The stonemason's work of the first intelligent men, who were presumably pupils of the tunnel constructors;

3. The gold and silver treasures of the Incas that were hidden here from the Spanish Conquistadores after 1532.

But the question of questions is:
Why were the tunnels built?

2: *The War of the Gods*

The first time I heard about a war in heaven was nearly thirty years ago when I was a little boy in the second form of the primary school at Schaffhausen. The master who taught religion told us that one day the archangel Lucifer had appeared before the Lord God and said: 'We are not going to serve you any longer.' So God ordered the mighty archangel Gabriel to destroy Lucifer and the rebels with a flaming sword.

Today I know that there is no mention of Lucifer in the Old Testament. It would be impossible, anyway, for the legendary figure of Moses, in whom the authors of the Old Testament are subsumed, is supposed to have lived about 1225 B.C., but Lucifer comes from Latin and that language is dated to 240 B.C. at the earliest. Lux fare (= Lucifer) means light-bringer, light-bearer, light-maker. It is odd that the sinister devil should be introduced into Catholic religious instruction as a bringer of light.

But the Old Testament does have something to say about war in heaven.

The reader will find descriptions of events and prophecies that have been preserved in chapters i–xxv of the Prophet Isaiah (740–701 B.C.). Isaiah xiv, 12, says:

> 'How art thou fallen from heaven, O Lucifer, son of the morning! how art thou cut down to the ground, which didst weaken the nations!
>
> For thou saidst in thine heart, I will ascend into heaven, I will exalt my throne above the stars of God: I will sit also upon the mount of the congregation, in the sides of the north.'

But we also find an unmistakable reference to strife in heaven in the New Testament. Revelation xii, 7–8, reads:

'And there was war in heaven: Michael and his angels fought against the dragon: and the dragon fought and his angels,
And prevailed not; neither was their place found any more in heaven.'

Many of the ancient documents of mankind mention wars and battles in heaven. The Book of Dzyan, a secret doctrine, was preserved for millennia in Tibetan crypts. The original text, of which nothing is known, not even whether it still exists, was copied from generation to generation and added to by initiates. Parts of the Book of Dzyan that have been preserved circulate around the world in thousands of Sanskrit translations, and experts claim that this book contains the evolution of mankind over millions of years. The Sixth Stanza of the Book of Dzyan runs as follows:

'At the fourth (round), the sons are told to create their images, one third refuses. Two obey. The curse is pronounced . . . The older wheels rotated downward and upward. The mother's spawn filled the whole. *There were battles fought between the creators and the destroyers, and battles fought for space;* the seed appearing and reappearing continuously. Make thy calculations, o disciple, if thou wouldst learn the correct age of thy small wheel.'

In the Egyptian Book of the Dead, that collection of texts which contained instructions for behaviour in the hereafter and was placed beside mummies in the tomb, Ra, the mighty Sun God, *fights with the rebellious children in the universe,* for Ra never left the world-egg during the battle. The Latin poet Ovid (43 B.C. to A.D. 17) is naturally better known to posterity for his *Ars amandi* than for his collection of myths, the *Metamorphoses*. In the latter, Ovid tells the story of Phaeton (= the shining one), who was once given permission by his father Helios, the Sun God, to drive the chariot of the sun. Phaeton could not control the chariot, fell through the sky and set the earth on fire. In Greek mythology the twelve children of Uranus (the personification of heaven) and Gaia (the personification of earth) play an important part. These twelve Titans were terrible children who used their tremendous strength to rebel against the established order, i.e. against Zeus, the king of the gods, and attacked Olympus, the abode of the gods. Hesiod (*circa* 700 B.C.), an earlier, Greek colleague of Ovid's, who recounts the ancestry of the gods and the origin of the world in his *Theogony*, tells us that the Titan Prometheus brought fire down to men from heaven after violent conflicts with Zeus. Zeus himself was forced to share world dominion with his brothers Poseidon and Hades after a bloodthirsty struggle. Referring to Zeus by his name of God of Light, Homer (*circa* 800 B.C.) describes him as cloud-banger, thunder-powerful and combative, who had no scruples about using lightning when fighting his enemies and so deciding the struggle in his favour. Lightning as a weapon also occurs in the Maori legends of the South Seas. They tell of a rebellion that broke out in heaven after Tane had arranged the stars. The legend names the rebels who were no longer willing to follow Tane, but Tane smote them with lightning, conquered the insurgents and threw them *down to earth*. Since then man has fought man, tribe fought tribe, animal fought animal and fish fought fish on this earth. The god Hinuno fares no better in the saga of the North American Payute Indians. After he had begun a battle with the gods, he was *thrown out of heaven*.

The International Academy for Sanskrit Research at

Mysore, India, had the courage to take a Sanskrit text by Maharishi Bharadvaya and replace the traditional conventional language of translation by words from our modern conceptual world. The result was staggering. The primaeval legends turned into a straightforward technical report! (*Gods from Outer Space.*)

If we apply the same procedure and simply replace the word 'heaven' by the modern concept 'universe', then in the twinkling of an eye the legends and myths of wars between the gods in heaven become gigantic battles in the universe between two hostile camps. In the children's heaven of religion, of course, no wars took place, in it reigned and still does reign the one and only beneficent and almighty God.

Yet the Old Testament mentions not just one god, but several gods:

> '... Let *us* make man in *our* image, after *our* likeness, and let them have dominion over the fish of the sea, and over the fowl of the air ...' (Genesis i, 26).

This *pluralis majestatis* is mentioned by the monotheistic Moses on another occasion:

> '... the sons of God saw the daughters of men that they were fair ...' (Genesis vi, 2).

Helene Petrovna Blavatsky (1831–1891), who founded the Theosophical Society in London in 1875, wrote in *The Secret Doctrine*, a work in six volumes, published in 1888:

> 'One of the names of the Jewish Jehova, "Sabaoth" or the "Lord of Hosts" (Isabaoth) belongs to the Chaldaean Sabaeans (or Tsabaeans) and has as its root the word "tsab", which means a "cart", a "ship" and an "army". So "sabaoth" literally means "the army of the ship", the "crew" or a "squadron of ships".'

I suspect that several gods had a hand in the creation
(= opening up) of the earth, as well as in the 'creation' of
man. The creation myth of the Quiché Mayas, the *Popol
Vuh*, tells us how man was created:

> 'It is said that those ones were created and shaped,
> they had no father, they had no mother, yet they were
> called men. They were not born of woman, they were
> not produced by creators and shapers, nor by Alom
> and Caholom, only by a miracle, by magic were they
> created and shaped . . .'

The Indian people of the Mayas, whose rather sudden
emergence into so-called history is dated to shortly after
the beginning of the Christian era, at first lived a very
primitive life in the forests, killing game with the most
rudimentary weapons. Yet the myths of the *Popol Vuh* are
supposed to date from this primitive stage. How could
phrases like the following have occurred to such primitive minds: '. . . they had no father, they had no mother
. . . they were not born of woman . . . by magic were
they created and shaped.'

It all seems so contradictory and confused that it
cannot be explained logically by existing theories. So I
should like to stimulate new ideas with the following
scenario.

If there were wars in the universe, there must have
been conquerors and conquered. The victors remained
in undisputed possession of their own planet, but the
defeated had to flee. They were forced to make for
another planet at very short notice in a still intact
spaceship. The reserves of energy and food that can be
carried in a spaceship last only for a limited time. So
the victors had only a definite period, which they knew,
in which to wipe out and annihilate the enemy. The

smallest advantage of time helped the defeated, because they could profit by time dilatation in their spaceship. (This phenomenon is scientifically proved. In a spaceship travelling just below the speed of light, time passes more slowly than on the launching planet, where it unfolds as usual.) The victors wanted no survivors. If only a couple of survivors reached a safe haven, they would produce offspring and grow into a race which would take revenge for their defeat. (If one couple had a knowledge of molecular biology—and the victors knew this—they could even alter primitive life on the planet that was their goal.) The conquered knew the 'mentality' of the conquerors and had the same technical know-how. So in a race against time they steered for the nearest planet. Did the defeated find the third planet out from the sun, our earth, 28,000 light years from the centre of the galaxy, after the war in the cosmos?

Was our blue planet the refuge of the losers in a cosmic battle?

If we continue to speculate about this theory, there are certain unavoidable premises. The home of the conquered must have had similar conditions to our earth. Their planet must have been about the same distance from the sun and naturally must have had an atmosphere containing oxygen.

What is the possibility that space flights could have begun from earthlike planets in the cosmos?

The statistical probability is enormous.

The fact that the question of the existence of cosmic neighbours has become a 'serious subject for research' (to quote Professor Hans Elsässer) is closely connected 'with the view of many natural scientists who find it ridiculous to assume that we are the only intelligent beings in the cosmos.'

Who knows how many stars there are?

We reckon there are 100 milliard fixed stars in our

galaxy. So that if every tenth fixed star is surrounded by a planetary system, ten milliard fixed stars have such systems. If we leave the majority of planets out of this rough calculation, taking only the figure of ten milliard fixed stars (which really implies a much larger number of planets) with one planet each and allotting earthlike qualities only to each tenth one, we arrive at the truly astronomical figure of one milliard planets resembling our earth. Supposing only each tenth planet to be of the size of the earth and possess the temperature range that makes it possible for life to originate and flourish, we are still faced with the inconceivable figure of 100,000,000! And even if we assume that only one in ten of these planets has a suitable atmosphere, we are still left with 10,000,000 planets with 'putative' conditions for organic life.

Hans F. Ebel of Heidelberg University writes in his essay 'Possible Life on Alien Planets':

'Astronomers' estimates tend to accept the figure of inhabitable earthlike planets in our Milky Way alone at hundreds of millions.'

So my theory does not inevitably collapse for lack of sites for launching ramps on earthlike planets. The hypertrophied opinion which dominated our conception of the world until a few years ago that the earth alone could support intelligent life has vanished from even the most rigid academic circles. *Tempi passati*.

There is one other question mark.

Supposing that the universe does teem with planets and intelligent life, might not all the forms of life on them have developed in quite different directions from those taken by organic life on earth? If, in addition to the tolerance allowed when making any high statistical estimate, we assume that the beings who waged their cosmic war were like humans, are we not being rather presumptuous? In fact, the most recent research in many fields related to the subject confirms that extra-terrestrial intelligences *must have been* like men. Atomic structures and chemical reactions are the same everywhere in the universe. And, according to Professor Heinz Haber:

'It is simply not true, as has often been imagined in the past, that the phenomenon of life waits patiently until inanimate nature creates on a planet conditions under which life can exist. It seems to be more likely that life, with its extraordinary chemical activity, contributes enormously to creating its own environment and can transform a planet in such a way that it is capable of supporting life in all its many-sided abundance.'

Lord Kelvin of Largs (1824–1907) was Professor at Glasgow University. In the natural sciences he had a great reputation as a physicist, for not only did he discover the second law of thermodynamics, but he also gave a strictly scientific definition of absolute temperature, which is measured in Kelvin degrees today. In addition, Kelvin discovered the standard formula for the length of oscillations in electric oscillatory circuits and the thermo-electric effect named after him. As clearly emerges from these brief biographical data, Lord Kelvin was an important figure in the exact natural sciences; he is held up to students as one of the really great men in his field. But nowadays we do not hear anything about Kelvin's conviction that in the very beginning 'life' did not originate on earth, our tiny planet, but came wafting from the remote depths of the universe in the form of spores. Kelvin was convinced that these unicellular vegetable spores—asexual germ cells, from which new life could originate—were so resistant to the intensest cold that they landed on earth still capable of creating life, together with meteors or meteoric dust, and developed under the life-giving power of light so that finally higher organisms could emerge from them. I advocate taking the whole Kelvin seriously, including the man who so many years ago rejected the arrogant assumption that life could only have originated on our planet. Even in these realms, which strictly pertain to natural science, we constantly come across the limits imposed by religious (= orthodox) thought. As life is finite, it must also be finite in the universe. Until natural scientists have *proved* that this conviction of Kelvin's is false, they should give it a privileged place in the broad spectrum of opinions about how life originated on earth. The noble Lord has earned that much.

I myself would never risk introducing such an audacious theory into the discussion. But I have come to the conclusion that the kind of speculative ideas for which I am attacked can be found by anyone who is prepared to do a little diligent reading in existing scientific literature. Comforting for me, discomforting for my critics.

For example, and this is important for my theory of war in the universe, I meet with scepticism if I try to use reproductions of cave drawings to prove that the recognisable accessories of space travel (spacesuits, antennae, supply systems, etc.) point to visits by intelligences from other stars. Nonsense, I am told. If equipment like that used today could be confirmed in such early times, the alien intelligences must have developed quite differently from ourselves. I never hear precise arguments, but —what must not be cannot be. Amid the vast sea of speculations there are some logical conclusions that give quite solid support for my theory that alien intelligences must have been the same as *homo sapiens*, or very like him.

Professor Roland Puccetti, a contributor to such well-known periodicals as *The Philosophical Quarterly* and *Analysis,* writes in his book *Extraterrestrial Intelligences from the Philosophical and Religious Point of View* that he made his study 'because after all the amateurish conclusions I felt it was high time to investigate the latest scientific findings in this field quite impartially, from the point of view of a philosophical and religious scholar.' Puccetti shares his opinion that intelligent beings throughout the universe must be more or less like *homo sapiens* with other eminent natural scientists. As early as 1964, the well-known biologist Dr Robert Bieri published the same conviction in 'Humanoids on Other Planets', a contribution to the *American Scientist*. After 15 years of research into enzymes, Dr Joseph Kraut, a biochemist at California University, came to the same conclusion.

But how can it be 'proved' that intelligent extra-terrestrial life developed similarly to man? The 'proof' can only be a logical sequence of conclusions based on demonstrable facts.

Professor Puccetti starts from the premise that similar external conditions lead to the formation of similar forms and organs in genetically different beings. This tendency exists on all earthlike planets where suitable conditions for complex forms of life occur. Therefore the differences in the evolution of beings that originated on our or any other planet should be minimal. For in all cases life began with the chemical transformation of the surface of the planet—'with the appearance of organic matter from inanimate matter on the basis of carbon compounds in a water medium'. It has been proved that herbivores and carnivores became differentiated in their oceanic environment and developed special forms 'before they conquered *terra firma*'. Fossils have not only been found in rock with an age of 60,000,000 years, but also in slate a milliard years old. The development of new kinds of bodies by formerly amphibious creatures was not a chance one. They needed different limbs in order to move about quickly on *terra firma*. Nature developed walking, which is the only sensible form of locomotion, because it is possible on any surface. Whereas amphibious creatures still had small brains, land creatures needed a larger thinking apparatus, because the dangers from their environment multiplied. But the larger brain was easier to carry and supply with blood in a walking position. What was the number of legs necessary for the new position, asks Puccetti? One leg would not be enough, because the animal would not be able to stand up again if it fell over. Uneven numbers would not have been practical, because balance would have been difficult. Yet several pairs would also have been unsuitable, because they would only have permitted slow crawling. Actually, fossil finds are clear proof that in the course of millions of years evolution steadily allowed the number of legs to atrophy, until finally two pairs proved to be the most suitable. 'Now two legs seem to be the ideal prerequisite for the development of a large brain, and with two pairs the necessary transformation of one pair into arms for the change over to life in the trees is made possible and the use of tools in the initial stage made easier.' It is illuminating that the transition from amphibious to terrestrial life necessitated such an alteration of the 'chassis'. If it was so with us, it was the same elsewhere in the universe. There is no longer any doubt that all life is of oceanic origin—on that point there should be general agreement. But still further modifications in the construction of the 'chassis' proved to be necessary. With the beginning of an active way of life as beasts of prey with two-sided symmetrical figures, the muzzle was placed at the front and the backside at the rear of the body. These two locations proved to be the most suitable for feeding and excreting in the case of hunting animals (and not only in their case!). In all beasts of prey the most important sensory organs and prehensile limbs are at the foremost part of the body near the muzzle. So it is no wonder that the brain, the biggest bundle of nerves, is also located there, for then orders from the brain can travel to the prehensile organs by the quickest route. Growing up on *terra firma* initiated a refinement of the nervous system that gradually produced the ability to formulate ideas. It is well known that dolphins 'have a sizeable brain, although they live in water. But the ability to formulate ideas seems only to emerge in connection with life in a community, with language and the use of tools.' As the use of even the simplest tools under water is extremely difficult, it is 'unlikely that a brain capable of conceptual thought could develop under these conditions, for the process requires a social environment and a certain form of objective speech.'—Professor Puccetti also excludes the possibility that intelligent beings elsewhere could be birdlike, because flying creatures must be light, whereas a large brain is heavy and needs a copious supply of blood. He mentions these variant forms of life to lead fantastic speculations about evolution back to more realistic lines of thought.

Another of the inevitable features of evolution is the similarity of the formation of the eye in widely different species of the animal world. They all have a perfect camera-like eye, with lens, retina, eye muscles, transparent cornea, etc. The number of eyes and their location are also identical. They are always in the head near the brain, just as the two ears are always in the most suitable place, at the highest part of the body. The senses of taste and smell developed with mouth and nose in the immediate vicinity of the nervous centre.

Professor Puccetti produces his proof, summarised briefly here, in order to refute the claim of biologists that technically intelligent life could have developed in an unlimited number of directions. For the claim that there are many different and controversial evolutionary possibilities denies that life *must* have developed into

intelligent forms in certain earthlike conditions on planets outside the solar system. Puccetti establishes—and
this is the thesis I have always upheld—that under extra-
terrestrial conditions similar to those on earth living
beings must have originated from the liquid medium,
water, and that they must inevitably have developed
according to the same patterns as on our earth, as soon
as they went on to dry land 'where it is possible for them
to develop a language, use tools and make the transition
to social forms of communal life.' This evolutionary path
must have been prescribed for intelligent life on all the
other planets. Moreover these developments in the universe have been so numerous, says Puccetti, that
attempts to contact intelligent extra-terrestrial beings
and communicate with them 'would not be doomed to
failure'. He continues: 'My conclusion is quite simply
this—that *intelligent extra-terrestrial beings throughout the
cosmos must, by and large, be similar to homo sapiens.*'

The circle closes. Lord Kelvin suspected that the first
form of life on our planet 'drifted over' from the universe!
Puccetti adduces from established knowledge about the
origin of all life that the laws of evolution were and are
the same everywhere. Joseph Kraut is convinced that
nature on other earth-like planets must have solved its
problems in the same way as it did in our case. And
Albert Einstein said that he wondered if nature did not
always play the same game.

If one can (or ought to) assume that intelligent life
exists on millions of other planets, the idea that this life
was (and is) older and therefore more advanced in every
way than terrestrial life is admittedly a speculation, but
not one to be rejected out of hand. Can't we bury the old
Adam as 'Lord of Creation' once and for all? Of course, I
cannot 'prove' my theory, but no one has produced arguments to convince me of the contrary. So I am going to
follow it through to the bitter end.

The rival parties in the cosmos had the same mathematical knowledge, the same standard of experience and shared a common stage of technological development. The defeated party, having escaped from the battle in a spaceship, had to make for a planet similar to their home, land there and organise a civilisation (in the absence of an existing one). They knew how great the danger of being located from the cosmos was and that the victors would use every kind of technical aid to seek them out. A game of hide-and-seek began, but a game in which their survival was at stake. The newly landed astronauts went underground. They dug themselves in, created subterranean communication routes over great distances and built strongpoints deep under the earth that afforded them safety, although they could emerge from them to cultivate areas of their new homeland and include them in the plans for a carefully thought out infrastructure.

I can refute the objection that the tunnel-builders must have 'betrayed' themselves by the enormous quantities of debris excavated while making the tunnels. As I credit them with an advanced technology, they were presumably equipped with a *thermal drill* of the kind described in *Der Spiegel* for 3 April, 1972, which reported it as the latest discovery.

The scientists of the U.S. Laboratory for Atomic Research at Los Alamos spent a year and a half developing the thermal drill. It has nothing in common with ordinary drills. The tip of the drill is made of wolfram and heated by a graphite heating element. There is no longer any waste material from the hole being drilled. The thermal drill melts the rock through which it bores and presses it against the walls, where it cools down. As *Der Spiegel* related, the first test-model bored almost soundlessly through blocks of stone 12 ft. thick. At Los Alamos they are now planning the construction of a thermal drill that is powered by a mini atomic reactor and eats into the earth like a mole, in the form of an armoured vehicle. This drill is intended to pierce the earth's crust, which is about 25 miles thick, and take samples of the molten magma that lies underneath it.

Ideas are duty-free, so I think it conceivable that the refugee astronauts were also able to use electron rays to build their tunnels. They had electrons 'vaporised' by a very hot cathode and then accelerated them in the electrical field between cathode and anode. They clustered the electron rays by means of a focussing electrode, i.e. all the 'vaporised' electrons were formed into a single ray. The American firm of Westinghouse has developed an electron ray generator for welding experiments in space. The electron ray is especially suitable for blasting rock, because the hardness of the rock is no obstacle to it. If an electron ray meets rock, it rips the thickest blocks apart by thermal tensions.

Did the tunnel makers possess a combination of thermal drills and electron ray guns? *It is perfectly possible.* If the drill came up against some exceptionally hard geological strata, these could be blasted by a few well-aimed shots with the gun. Then the armoured thermal drill would attack the resulting blocks and heat the mass of debris to the liquid state. As soon as the liquid rock cooled down, it would form a diamond-hard glaze. The tunnel system would be safe against infiltration by water, and supports for the chambers would be superfluous.

I was stimulated to make these speculations by the tunnel system in Ecuador. Juan Moricz thinks that the long straight galleries in particular have glazed walls (fig. 19) and that the large rooms were made by blasting. Neatly blasted layers of rock are clearly recognisable at the tunnel entrance, as is the right-angled door blown out of the rock face. (Fig. 20.) The stratification of the stone slabs and the stones assembled in the normal way

Fig. 19. Juan Moricz claims that the long passages have glazed walls and that explosives were used to blast out the big halls.

for building houses cannot have been introduced into the construction naturally, for example by an inrush of water. The technical care with which the tunnel system was planned is proved by the ventilation shafts that recur at regular intervals (fig. 21). These shafts are all accurately worked and on an average are between 5 ft. 10 ins. and 10 ft. long and 2 ft. 7 ins. wide. Swarms of buzzard-like birds (fig. 22) leave the dark labyrinth through these shafts, coming and going all day long, and finally returning to die in the dungeon.

It was here, in the impenetrable depths, that the 'gods' decided to create men 'in their image', many years later, when they were no longer afraid of being discovered.

The *Popol Vuh*, the sacred scriptures of the Quiché Indians, a branch of the great Maya family that lived in Central America, tells us about this 'creation':

Fig. 20. A tunnel entrance 360 ft. below ground level. Neatly blasted layers of stone are as clearly recognisable as the right-angled door 'shot' into the rock. The pieces of stone (right) placed as in normal house-building cannot have originated naturally. When it was being built, it must have been higher. An inrush of water at some time caused a fall of rubble.

'But the name of the place to which Balam Quitze, Balam Acab and Iqui Balam came was the caves of Tula, seven caves, seven gorges. The Tamub and Ilocab came there, too. This was the name of the town where they received their gods . . . In turn they left the gods behind and Hacavitz was the first . . . Mahucutah also left his god behind. But Hacavitz was not hidden in the forest—Hacavitz disappeared into a bare mountain . . .'

And now comes the passage from the *Popol Vuh* already quoted. I cannot resist quoting it again in this connection, because of its astonishing contents:

'It is said that those ones were created and shaped, they had no father, they had no mother, yet they were

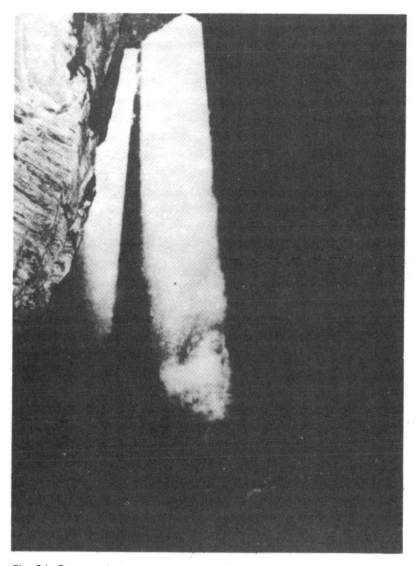

Fig. 21. One regularly comes across artificial ventilation shafts like this. They are 5 ft. 10 ins. to 10 ft. long and 2 ft. 7 ins. wide.

Fig. 22. The number of buzzard-like birds living in the underground tunnels is legion. They are constantly coming in and out of the ventilation shafts, but finally return to the labyrinth to die.

called men. They were not born of woman, they were not produced by creators and shapers, nor by Alom and Caholom, only by a miracle, by magic were they created and shaped . . .'

A cuneiform tablet from Nippur, the town in Central Babylonia which was the seat of the Sumerian god Enlil in the third millennium B.C., has this account of the origin of man:

'In those days, in the creation chamber of the gods, in their house Duku were Lahar and Ashman formed . . .'

Here it might be objected that the parallels between the text of the *Popol Vuh* and the cuneiform inscription from Nippur are somewhat far-fetched, for it is about 8,000 miles as the crow flies from Central America, the homeland of the Mayas, to the fertile crescent between the Euphrates and the Tigris, the home of the Sumerians! But this is no carefully selected parallel from two cultural entities widely separated in space and time. It is well known that the Old Testament, especially the Pentateuch, contains a good many Sumerian concepts. What is not so well known is that the Old Testament and the *Popol Vuh* also have just as many obvious features in common, and even more hidden ones. Let sceptics compare the following passages:

'And the whole earth was of one language and of one speech.' (Genesis xi, 1.)
'There they saw the rising of the sun. They had a single language. They prayed to neither wood nor stone . . .' (*Popol Vuh*.)

'And Moses stretched out his hand over the sea: and the Lord caused the sea to go back by a strong east wind all that night, and made the sea dry land, and the waters were divided.

And the children of Israel went into the midst of the sea upon the dry ground: and the waters were a wall unto them on their right hand, and on their left.' (Exodus xiv, 21–22.)

'They hardly noticed how they crossed the sea. They traversed it as if there had been no sea; they crossed it on stones. Round stones rose from the sand and they walked across on the rows of stones. The place was called shifting sand; those who crossed *the sea that divided itself* gave it the name. That is how they came over.' (*Popol Vuh.*)

'. . . This is the token of the covenant which I make between me and you and every living creature that is with you . . .' (Genesis ix, 12.)

'This will succour ye when ye call upon me. This is the sign of the covenant. But now I have to go, with a heavy heart . . .' (*Popol Vuh.*)

'Then these men were bound in their coats, their hosen, and their hats, and their other garments, and were cast into the midst of the burning fiery furnace . . .

'He answered and said, Lo, I see four men loose, walking in the midst of the fire, and they have no hurt; and the form of the fourth is like the Son of God.' (Daniel iii, 21 and 25.)

'Then those men went into the fire, into a fire house. Within it all was red hot, but they were not consumed by fire. Smooth of body and fair of face they appeared in the twilight. The people in the places they had passed through had wished them dead. But that did not come to pass. Then consternation seized those from Xibalba.' (*Popol Vuh.*)

The reader is entitled to ask what this detour taking in a Sumerian cuneiform inscription, the Old Testament and the *Popol Vuh* has to do with my tunnel builders. I am trying to produce arguments for my conviction that in the very beginning *there was only one source of the origin of homo sapiens*, namely the spacemen who first made the mutation. Only much later, when peoples and races had settled in other parts of the globe, were *new* experiments in *new* places introduced into the first primordial tradition. But the *core* of the act of creation, namely that the gods created the first men in their own image, is preserved in all the world-wide traditions! The creation of man by extra-terrestrial intervention does not interfere with the theory of our ancestry or the theory of evolution.

Now there are two questions. Firstly, what event set off the process of becoming man? Secondly, why did *homo sapiens* alone of all the kinds of hominids become intelligent?

There are many answers, but none of them is convincing. About a million years ago all hominid types of ape had a brain capacity of about 25 cubic inches. If the climate drove the apes down from the trees during the following millennia, that must have included all kinds of apes and not just the one which was selected to produce *homo sapiens*. But if the ability to produce tools had been a prerequisite for development and further evolution, there should not really be any apes left today. 'Is it absolutely essential to become man in order not to die out?' asks Oskar Kiss Maerth in his book *Der Anfang war das Ende* (The Beginning was the End). With regard to the problem of the origin of man, Maerth puts exciting questions like this:

'If one race of monkeys was forced to stand on its hind legs for fear of wild animals and because it was easier to feed themselves, why did not the other apes, too, stand on *their* hind legs, for the same reason?

Basically all hominid apes were and are veg-
etarian...

So were man's ancestors; they only became meat
eaters during the process of becoming man ... Meat
eating is supposed to have been a sign of increased
intelligence and therefore an advance, because man
could nourish himself "better" and "more easily" on
meat. For this compliment thank the wolves and wild
cats, who had been carnivores many millions of years
before.

Why did meat eating suddenly become an "easier"
form of nourishment for man's ancestors? Since when
has it been easier to kill a gazelle or a bison than to
pluck fruit from a tree?

During the last million years many dry and rainy
periods alternated ... all the great apes were able to
withdraw to the remaining woods to continue leading
their usual way of life. Why did all the great apes do
this, except those from which man is supposed to have
originated later?'

There is really nothing in the theory of evolution to
explain the mighty leap by which *homo sapiens* set himself
apart from his family of hominids. All we hear is that the
brain suddenly became efficient, acquired technical
know-how, was capable of observing the heavens and
establishing communication in social communities. In
terms of the history of evolution this leap from anima-
listic being to *homo sapiens* took place over night. A
miracle? Miracles just don't happen.

The assertion that the intelligence of our earliest
ancestors had already begun a million years ago and
developed nice and slowly once they lived in communities does not hold water. All mammals live in groups,
flocks and herds; they hunt and defend themselves

communally. Have they become intelligent on this account? Even if a being resembling man has produced primitive tools, that in itself does not make him a *homo sapiens*. Professor Leakey of the National Research Centre for Prehistory and Palaeontology, Nairobi, refers to finds near Fort Ternan, which showed that *Kenyapithecus Wickeri* produced edged tools and that *homo habilis* used simple tools two million years ago. Leakey also tells us that Jane van Lavich-Goodall investigated chimpanzees in their natural surroundings and established that these distant cousins of man regularly make and use a variety of simple tools. Who is willing to admit these chimpanzees, which meet the criteria for membership of *homo sapiens*, into the circle of intelligent human beings?

Beings resembling man that made and used tools have always existed. Beings resembling man who worshipped and feared the gods, painted cave walls with frescoes, sang songs, had a feeling of shame, cultivated friendship and buried their fellow-men—*those kinds* of beings have not existed for so long. I doubt if they ever would have existed without artificial mutation by extra-terrestrial visitors. So I hazard the claim that the vanquished in a cosmic battle first set the process of becoming man in motion with their knowledge of the genetic code by means of an artificial mutation.

On 5 June, 1972, the Associated Press, Washington, distributed a news item on the 129-page report of the Committee for Astronomical Research of the American Academy of Science. In the view of these scholars the probability of intelligent extra-terrestrial civilisations existing in the universe has increased considerably during the last seven years. The Academy recommends that attempts by astronomers to discover such distant worlds with intelligent inhabitants should be supported by large government subsidies. Admittedly existing telescopes could already receive radio signals from extra-terrestrial civilisations, but new instruments must be developed capable of picking up signals from inhabited heavenly bodies outside our solar system as well. The committee's report says literally:

> 'At this very moment radio waves carrying the conversations of beings living vast distances away may be reaching us. Perhaps we could record these conversations if only we directed a radio telescope in the right direction and tuned in to the right frequency.'

Insofar as one can produce indications in support of a theory, I think one should introduce them into a serious discussion. It is not a question of asking for *proofs*. What scientific theory could be built up on proofs from its first conception?

Nor is it a question of a 'substitute religion', as many critics claim. If my theories smack of a substitute religion, then logically scientific first-borns, whose embryos were theories, must also have been 'substitute religions' to begin with. The average man cannot carry out the series of experiments which ought to lead to the proof of a theory. Should he or must he *believe* in scientific theories even if the results of research finally show them to be wrong? I want to stimulate thought with my theories. No more, but also no less. And here I have put forward my new theories, stimulated by indications of how the tunnels in Ecuador and Peru could have originated and when *homo sapiens* may have celebrated his 'birthhour'.

I leave it to the scientific world to answer me.

3: *Traces of the Gods in China, Too*

The China Airlines Boeing had taken off from Singapore an hour behind schedule and had only made up half an hour when it landed in Taipeh at 15.30 hrs. And I had arranged a meeting with Mr Chiang Fu-Tsung, Director of the National Palace Museum, for 17.00 hrs.

I left my luggage at the Ambassador Hotel in Nanking East Road, hailed a taxi, got in next to the friendly laughing driver and said: 'To the National Palace Museum, please.' The skinny little Buddha next to me smiled, but I had a strong feeling that he had not understood what I said. As he drove along at breakneck speed, I described my destination in all the languages I knew. My Buddha nodded indulgently, put his foot on the accelerator and finally stopped—outside the railway station! He whipped open the door smartly and with a radiant smile pointed to the station, which was obviously not the museum I was looking for. If only I had known a few words of Chinese! I went into the main hall and suddenly I had a brainwave. In the middle of it there was a bookstall with hundreds of post-cards on sale showing all the interesting buildings in Taipeh and Taiwan. I bought post-cards of all the places I intended to visit during the next few days. My Buddha nodded earnestly when I showed him the beautiful museum building and drove back the same way we had come. The museum was quite close to my hotel! (Fig. 23.)

I knew that there would be no language difficulties with Mr Chiang Fu-Tsung, who had studied in Berlin and spoke German.

I had been told this by Mr Chi, proprietor of the best

71

Fig. 23. With the help of a picture post-card my skinny Buddha drove me to the lovely Palace Museum in Taipeh to meet Mr Chiang Fu-Tsung.

Chinese restaurant I have ever eaten in, the Lu-Taipeh in Lucerne. Mr Chi spent most of his life as chef to Chiang Kai-Shek, before he decided to become a restaurateur in Switzerland. My friend Chi knew that I was obsessed with the desire to find out as much as I could about the mysterious finds at Baian Kara Ula.

That was the site in the Sino-Tibetan frontier zone where the Chinese archaeologist Chi Pu Tei found 716 granite plates in 1938. They were 2 cm. thick, with a hole exactly in the centre from which a double-tracked grooved script ran out spirally to the edge of the plate. In fact they were rather like our longplaying records. Brilliant scholars puzzled for years over the secret of the stone plates until Professor Tsum Um Nui of the

Academy of Prehistory, Peking, succeeded in deciphering part of the grooved scripts in 1962. Geological
analysis showed a considerable cobalt and metal content; physicists established that all the plates had a high
vibration rhythm, which led to the conclusion that they
had been exposed to high electrical tensions at some
time. The finds at Baian Kara Ula became a sensation
when the Russian philologist Dr Vyacheslav Saizev published some deciphered texts of the stone plates. They related that 12,000 years ago members of an alien people
landed on the third planet, but their aircraft no longer
had enough power to take off from that distant world. I
have established these proven facts in detail in *Gods from
Outer Space*.

But the reason for my journey to Taiwan was that the
news published in Moscow, the scholar's full report on
the stone plates, was deposited both in the Peking Academy and the Historical Archives at Taipeh.

Thanks to a letter from my friend Chi, I had an
appointment on this cold wet January afternoon with the
Director of the Palace Museum, who had confirmed our
meeting in a courteous letter before I had even started on
my third journey round the world.

The chances of my getting on the track of the stone
plates in the Palace Museum seemed very good. The precious collection, with more than 250,000 catalogued
items, had been moved from its original home in
Peking on several occasions during the last 60 years. In
1913, during the uprising of the Kuomintang Party, in
1918, during the Civil War, in 1937, during the war
with the Japanese, who occupied Peking, and in 1947,
when Mao Tse Tung founded the People's Republic of
China with the People's Army of Liberation and made
Peking the capital again. Since 1947 the art treasures
have been stored in Taipeh.

A decorative visiting card on which Mr Chi had

written greetings and recommendations to his friend
Chiang Fu Tsung with a fine brush made smiling men in
uniform silently open all doors till we reached the
Director's office. He greeted me in German—only when
I apologised for being late did he wave my excuses away
with a long sentence in Chinese. (Fig. 24.)

Fig. 24. I had several productive and interesting conversations with Mr
Chiang Fu-Tsung, the Director of the Palace Museum.

'You are a friend of my friend, you are my friend. Wel-
come to China. What can I do for you?' he asked. As we
approached a low table, he gave an order aloud—to
whom? Even before we could sit down, museum guards
brought paper-thin porcelain cups and a decorated pot
full of herb tea. The Director filled our cups.

I went straight to the point and said that I was interested in the Baian Kara Ula finds and that I should like

to see the scholar's report on the stone plates that was here in Taipeh. My enthusiasm was dampened when Mr Chiang explained that this extensive report had not shared the Museum's odyssey, but was still preserved in the Peking Academy, with which he had no contact. He noticed my intense disappointment, but could give me very little consolation with the rest of his information.

'I know about your efforts. They delve deeply into the prehistory of peoples. I can only help with our primaeval ancestor Sinanthropus, who was discovered in 1927 in the valley of Choukoutien, 25 miles south-west of Peking. In the opinion of the anthropologists, this Sinanthropus Pekinensis, Peking Man, is similar to homo Heidelbergicnsis, but in any case resembles the Chinese race, as it exists today in 800,000,000 examples. Peking Man is supposed to come from the Middle Pleistocene, i.e. to be about 400,000 years old. After that there is really no more prehistory.'

The Director explained that there was no further evidence of Neolithic cultures in North China until the third millennium B.C. when the Yang-Shao culture on the Huang Ho produced painted ribbon pottery. About the second millennium B.C. came the Ma-Shang culture, the black pottery culture and the stone and copper culture of Sheng Tse Ai of Shantung, followed by the luxuriant decoration which came in with the beginning of the Bronze Age with the *t'ao t'ieh*, or monster mask, and Li Wen with its broken right-angled representations of thunder. From the fifteenth to the eleventh centuries there was a highly developed script with more than 2,000 pictographic and symbolic characters which were used for oracular inscriptions. In all periods, it was the task of Chinese rulers, the 'Sons of Heaven', to see that the course of nature unfolded in an orderly manner.

'As far as I know, for I am not a prehistorian, there is nothing in the Middle Kingdom to lend wings to your special fantasy, no stone axes, no primitive tools, not even traces of cave paintings. And the oldest inscribed bones were dated to 3000 B.C.'

'What was on the bones?'

'So far it has proved impossible to decipher the inscriptions.'

'Isn't there anything else?'

'A single vase that was excavated at An-yang near Honan. It was dated to 2800 B.C.'

'Excuse me, Mr Chiang, but surely China must have some evidence of its prehistory. There must be something to show the development from the prehistorical to the historical period. Are there no mysterious ruins, no crumbled cyclopean walls?'

'Our Chinese history can be traced back without a gap to the Emperor Huang Ti and he lived in 2698 B.C. It is a known fact that the compass existed as early as that. Therefore time cannot have begun with Huang Ti! But what happened before him, my dear friend, lies in the stars.'

'What do you mean, in the stars?'

Was there a tit-bit left for me in this conversation after all? There was. Mr Chiang smiled:

'From the very earliest times the dragon has always been the Chinese symbol of divinity, inaccessibility and invincibility. P'an Ku (fig. 25) is the legendary name of the constructor of the Chinese universe. He created the earth out of granite blocks which he caused to fly down out of the cosmos. He divided up the waters and made a gigantic hole in the sky. He divided the sky into the eastern and western hemispheres.'

'Might he have been a heavenly regent, who appeared in the firmament in a spaceship?'

'No, my friend, the legend says nothing about spaceships, it only mentions dragons, but it describes P'an Ku as he who mastered chaos in the universe. He created the

Yin Yang, the conception of the dual forces in nature. Yang stands for male power and the heavens, Yin for

Fig. 25. Chinese brush drawing of the God P'an Ku, legendary master of chaos and constructor of the Chinese universe. He is supposed to have built the world out of granite blocks that flew down from space.

female beauty and the earth. Everything that happens in the cosmos or on earth is subordinate to one of these two symbols, which have penetrated deeply into Chinese cosmological philosophy.'

According to legend, every ruler and 'Son of Heaven' is supposed to have lived for 18,000 terrestrial years and if we take this estimate at its face-value, P'an Ku brought order into the heavens 2,229,000 years ago! Perhaps these astronomical calculations may be a few years out here and there, but what does it matter with such a family tree?

P'an Ku, whose legend is said to have spread throughout China, was depicted differently in different regions, which is not surprising in view of the vast size of this country with its surface area of 3,800,000 sq. miles. Sometimes he is a being with two horns on his head and a hammer in his right hand, sometimes he appears as a dragon mastering the four elements, sometimes he holds the sun in one hand and the moon in the other, sometimes he is chipping away at a rock-face, watched by a snake.

Actually, the P'an Ku legend in China is probably not so old as the mighty man himself. Travellers from the kingdom of Siam (Thailand) are reputed to have brought the legend to China for the first time in the sixth century.

'Chinese mythology describes Yan Shih Tien-Tsun as the "father of things",' said the Director. 'He is the unfathomable being, the beginning and end of all things, the highest and most inconceivable being in heaven. In later times he was also called Yu Ch'ing. If you write about him, you must take care not to confuse Yu Ch'ing with the mysterious Emperor Yu, who is reputed to have caused the Flood. Do you know the legend of Yan Shih Tien-Wang?'

I shook my head. The Director took a volume of the Dictionary of Chinese Mythology from his shelves.

'There, read the story in your hotel. You will find some stories in the dictionary that are fascinating when considered in connection with your theories. For example, the legend of the goddess Chih Nu who was the patron saint of weavers. While she was still young, her father sent her to a neighbour who kept watch over the "Silver Stream of the Heavens", obviously the Milky Way. Chih Nu grew up and became very beautiful. She spent the days and nights playing and laughing, never was there a wilder or crazier lover in heaven than Chih Nu. The Sun

King grew tired of these goings-on and when she bore a child to her guardian friend, he ordered the ardent lover to take up his post at the other end of the Silver Stream and only to see the lovely Chih Nu once a year on the seventh night of the seventh month.'

'The story of the king's children who could not meet each other!'

'The legend has a happy ending for the lovers. Millions of shining heavenly birds formed an endless bridge over the Milky Way. So Chih Nu and her guardian could meet whenever they wanted.'

'If the shining heavenly birds were really spaceships patrolling between the stars, it seems perfectly plausible for the lovers to have met as often as they wished.'

Mr Chiang Fu-Tsung stood up:

'You *are* a visionary! But of course you're not forced to kow-tow to traditional explanations. Perhaps modern interpretations of myths and legends are justified, perhaps they will throw new light on things. There is a lot we don't know yet.'

The Director appointed the best-informed member of his staff, Marshal P. S. Wu, Head of the Excavation Department, to act as my guide during my stay. Although only a fraction of the 250,000 items in the Museum are on display at any one time, there is still such a bewilderingly large number that I could scarcely have collected my 'finds' without the help of Mr Wu who understood instinctively what interested me. Here is a selection:

Bronze vessels from the period of the Shang dynasty (1766–1122 B.C.) automatically reminded me of the other side of the Pacific. Nazca pottery, pre-Inca work much more recent than the Chinese vessels, exhibits very similar ornaments: geometrical lines, opposed squares and spirals.

A jade axe, a small copy of a larger one. The divine symbol of the dragon with a trail of fire is engraved on the greenish stone; the firmament is decorated with spheres. I remembered identical representations on Assyrian cylinder seals.

Altar trappings for the worship of the god of the mountains and clouds is the orthodox archaeological label under a right-angled object dating to 206 B.C. A mountain is visible, but it is dwarfed by a giant sphere with a trail of fire. This sphere, which has three small spheres arranged geometrically above it, is so big that it seems to be quite unrelated to sun, moon and stars. Altar trappings? It is far more likely that in the remote past this picture recalled some unforgettable, incomprehensible phenomenon in the sky.

Jade discs (fig. 26) with a diameter of 2¾ to 6½ ins. They have holes in the middle like gramophone records. They are held upright against 7¾ inch-high obelisks by pegs. Once again I do not believe the archaeologists when they say that these ceremonial discs were divine symbols of power and strength, and the obelisks phallic symbols. I was fascinated by the jade discs, many of which had neatly milled sharp angles like those on toothed wheels round their circumference. Is there some connection between these so-called ceremonial discs and the stone plates from Baian Kara Ula? If we accept that the plates from the Sino-Tibetan border region were models for the ceremonial discs, the veil enshrouding the mystery would be lifted. After a visit to the Baian Kara Ula region by the astronauts who made the plates, presumably for transmitting information, reverent priests imagined that they would be doing work pleasing to God or even acquire some of the qualities of the brilliantly clever beings who had vanished simply by making discs like those that the strangers had used. That would square with the current archaeological explanation of the

discs, for by this roundabout route they actually could
have become religious trappings.

Fig. 26. The jade discs have a hole in the middle and often sharp points
like those on toothed wheels round the circumference. Were they made
from models?

Dr Vyacheslav Saizev, who published important data
about the stone plates, found a rock painting (fig. 27)
near Fergana, in Uzbekistan, not far from the Chinese
frontier. Not only does the figure wear an astronaut's
helmet, not only can we identify breathing apparatus,
but in his hands, isolated by the spaceman's suit, he
holds a plate of the kind found by the hundred at Baian
Kara Ula!

One day I picked up the Dictionary of Chinese
Mythology and read the legend of Yuan Shih Tien
Wang, which I reproduce here in abbreviated form:

'In a long past age the ancient sage Yuan Shih Tien

Wang lived in the mountain on the edge of the eternal ice. He told stories about olden times in such picturesque language that those who heard him believed

Fig. 27. Dr Vyacheslav Saizev found this rock painting near Fergana, in Uzbekistan. An astronaut holds a disc, similar to those found by the hundred at Baian Kara Ula. A recording?

that Yuan Shih himself had been present at all the wonderful events. One of his listeners, Chin Hung, asked the sage where he had lived before he had come to the mountain. Without a word, Yuan Shih raised both arms until they pointed to the stars. Then Chin Hung wanted to know how he could find his way in the infinite void of the heavens. Yuan Shih kept silent, but two gods in shining armour appeared and Chin

Hung, who was present, told his people that one god had said: "Come, Yuan Shih, we must go. We shall wander through the darkness of the universe and travel past distant stars to our home." '

Taipeh, the capital of Formosa (or Taiwan) and Nationalist China, has nearly two million inhabitants, universities, high schools and exceptionally well-run museums. From its main port of Keelung products such as sugar, tea, rice, bananas, pineapples (which flourish in the tropical monsoon climate), wood, camphor and fish are exported. Since Taiwan, with a population of 13,000,000, became an independent country in 1949, its industry has grown at a fantastic rate, so that today textiles, all kinds of engines, agricultural machinery, electrical goods, etc., with Made in Taiwan stamped on them, are loaded on to ships for customers all over the world. The government encourages the mining of gold, silver, copper and coal, which brings in foreign exchange.

Once again it is not clear whence and when the original Mongolian inhabitants, the Paiwan, came to the island. Today a quarter of a million of them live in seven different tribes in the most inaccessible part of the mountain range, where they were driven by successive waves of Chinese invaders. Only a generation ago, Paiwan warriors showed their bravery by head-hunting; today they hunt game in their mountain fastness. The tribes have survived in a remarkably pure state; they live according to the unchanging laws of nature. Their way of reckoning time is as simple as their way of life. The day begins at cockcrow; its passage is measured by the length of the shadows. The new year is recognised when the mountain plants start to blossom, its high point when the fruit ripens, its end with the first snow which cuts the tribes off from the world completely. From very early times, the Paiwans have practised monogamy, so it is unimportant whether a suitor buys or abducts his bride, or woos her bashfully, the only thing that matters is that he keeps her for life. The Paiwan's favourite stimulant is betel, which he manufactures in his own homemade 'laboratory' from the nutmeg-like fruits of the betel palm, with the addition of burnt lime and a good pinch of betel pepper. Betel tastes as bitter as gall, but is supposed to be refreshing. As betel turns spittle red and teeth blue-black, the friendly grin of a Paiwan warrior is frightening rather than reassuring. If I had not been reliably assured that they no longer practise head-hunting, I would have beaten a hasty retreat, because I need my head a little longer.

The Museum of the Province of Taipeh possesses a unique collection of Paiwan wood carvings. Their wood sculptures are considered to be the last examples of a dying folk art. They preserve primaeval motifs from

Fig. 28. The chieftain lived here! The two floating figures to the left of the four concentric circles wear the classical aprons of prehistoric astronauts to be found on many monoliths.

sagas and legends that have been handed down for many many generations.

The man who seeks for gods will find them.

Hanging in the museum was a piece of wood 28 ins. wide by 10 ins. high. (Fig. 28.) Once upon a time, when hung on a hut, it meant: the chief lives here! To the left of the four striking concentric circles *float* two figures, who are wearing the by now classical 'aprons' of pre-historic astronauts, of the kind to be found, for example, on the Toltec monoliths (fig. 29) in the Museum für Völkerkunde in Berlin. Both figures are wearing a kind of overall, and shoes. The being on the left wears a helmet and extended ultra-short-wave antennae.

A wooden sculpture (fig. 30) represents a being with large genital organs, whose head is protected by a close-fitting helmet. A small triangle is engraved on the helmet, perhaps the emblem of his astronautical forma-tion. A snake twines round his helmet. Symbol of loathsomeness in biblical times, in the sagas of the Mayas the snake rose again into the air as a 'feathered creature', and now it crops up again here among forgot-ten tribes in the mountain ranges of Formosa. All over the world we find snakes, flying snakes, in traditional popular art! Why did the Paiwan paint their canoes (fig. 31) with snakes, why are the heads of the 'divine figures' round like helmets, why are they in (antenna) contact with each other and why do the contacts end in a 'sun' with a series of toothed wheels inside it? Why do snakes (fig. 32), twined round stars, gaze steadily heavenwards with their triangular heads? Why does a Paiwan god hold a snake that passes above him and his helmet? Why in particular is a *female* goddess (fig. 34) concealed in a mask, why does she wear clumsy goggles and why is there a snake above and around her head? Obviously this outfit was never chic, but it was suitable for a spaceflight and the snake symbolised a limit to cosmic flight.

Fig. 29. Toltec monoliths in the Museum für Völkerkunde, Berlin. The left-hand picture is entitled 'Ode to the Sun God'. It comes from *Gods from Outer Space*. The right-hand one is my own photograph from the American Museum in Madrid, which has plaster casts of the original. The important thing is the 'aprons', for the Paiwan tribe of Formosa scratch the same aprons on wood and stone when depicting their own gods. Were they part of astronauts' uniforms?

Fig. 30. This figure has a ray gun in his hand, like those in the pictures of the gods at Val Camonica, Italy, and Monte Alban, Mexico. And a snake is coiled round his helmet. A space symbol.

Fig. 31. Why did the Paiwan paint their canoes with frescoes of the gods, like the ancient Egyptians? What do the figures' linking up antennae mean?

All this should be interpreted in terms of early religions, say the archaeologists. They say that snakes were divine 'symbols of reverence'. If so, why did not the Paiwans use fish, sharks, waves or turtles as models, when they painted their canoes with symbols of religious provenance? Why did not the chief pin a shield that bore the sign of his tribe (there were some beautiful ones) on the wall of his house?

The carvings, which are often half-rotten, are extremely lovely. They all have concentric circles and spirals, and they continually emphasise the connection between man and snake, with the snake always hissing heavenwards *above* the figure. Frequently the figures are carved in a floating, as opposed to a standing position, as if they were weightless. I do not think such reproductions were the products of artistic imagination. The first ancestors of the Paiwan must have seen that it was possible for beings to *float* in the air and told their descendants so. The Paiwan are still primitive even today. In their masterly carvings they represent both *real* things from their environment and also the stereotypes which come from a kind of collective unconscious going back to time immemorial. Their contemporary woodwork shows that the Paiwan carvers are quite up to date. They perpetuate men in Japanese uniforms, with their weapons. They have *seen these men*. They are not straining their imaginations. They have never done so; in all ages they represented what they had actually seen in artistically perfect combination with traditional motifs.

An especially remarkable motif is a three-headed being flying in a snake—a motif that recurs in a silk manuscript of the Chou culture (1122–236 B.C.).

Fig. 32. Snakes coiling round stars with their triangular heads staring heavenwards. On a Paiwan wooden tablet.

Mr Y. C. Wang, Director of the Historical Museum, Taipeh, showed me round his collection of representations of mythological beings, half men, half animals, often with bird's heads on winged bodies, parallels to the

Fig. 33. This wooden sculpture shows a god with a tight-fitting helmet and once again a snake, the ancient emblem of the space traveller.

Assyrian and Babylonian winged gods. Seals from the Chou period are as numerous as the rings in a jeweller's showcase. Up to 1 cm. in size they do not appear to have been simply decorative ornaments. Under my magnifying glass, they looked remarkably like integrated circuits.

There were also some 'bronze mirrors' from $2\frac{3}{4}$ ins. to 5 ins. in diameter engraved with symbols and characters that have been partially deciphered.

The translated text of an engraved inscription from the Chou dynasty reads:

'Wherever suns shine, there is life.'

For amusement's sake, I have reproduced the square

in the centre of this bronze mirror (fig. 35) in comparison with two integrated circuits from the firm of Siemens.

The geologist Thuinli Lynn told me about a discovery that is unknown to the western world.

Fig. 34. Paiwan goddess in a space traveller's mask. She holds a snake, symbol of the universe, in her hands.

During excavations in the 'Valley of Stones' in July, 1961, Chi Pen Lao, Professor of Archaeology in the University of Peking, came across an underground cave system. At a depth of 105 ft. he found entrances to a labyrinth in the spurs of the Honan mountains, on the south shore of Lake Tung Ting, west of Yoyang. He located passages that undoubtedly led under the lake. The passage walls were smooth and glazed. The walls of one hall, into which several passages led, were covered with paintings. They represented animals, all fleeing in one direction, driven by men who held 'blow-pipes' to

Fig. 35. 'Wherever suns shine, there is life,' reads the inscription on a bronze mirror. Engravings like those on this mirror could easily be taken for modern integrated circuits!

their lips. Above the fleeing animals, and this is the sensational part of the account as far as I am concerned, flies a shield on which stand men holding weapon-like implements which they are aiming at the animals. The men on the 'flying shield', says Mr Chi Pen Lao, wear modern jackets and long trousers. Mr Lynn thinks that scholars have probably succeeded in establishing the date when the tunnel was built, but news from Red China only emerges sparingly and after long delays.

The report of the 'flying shield' and the men aiming at the animals from above at once reminded me of a museum piece which had left an indelible impression on my memory. It was the skeleton of a bison (fig. 36), whose brow had been pierced by a neat shot, and I had seen it in the Museum of Palaeontology in Moscow.

The original home of the bison was Russian Asia. The age of my fossil bison was dated to the Neolithic (8000 to 2700 B.C.), when weapons were still made by flaking stones, and the most modern weapon created in that period was the stone axe. A blow with a stone axe would inevitably have shattered the bison's skull, but under no circumstances could it have left a bullet hole. A firearm in the Neolithic? In fact, the idea seems so absurd that the experts could dismiss it with a wave of the hand, if it were not for the fact that the Neolithic marksman's bison trophy is on show in Moscow.

On the eleventh and last day of my stay in Taipeh, President Ku Cheng Kang, Member of the National Assembly, gave a dinner for me. I was surrounded by distinguished politicians and scholars: B. Hsieh, Professor at Fuyen University, Shun Yao, still UNESCO Secretary-General representing the Republic in January, 1972, Hsu Chih Hsin and Shuang Jeff Yao of the Public Relations Department, Senyung Chow of the Government and of course my

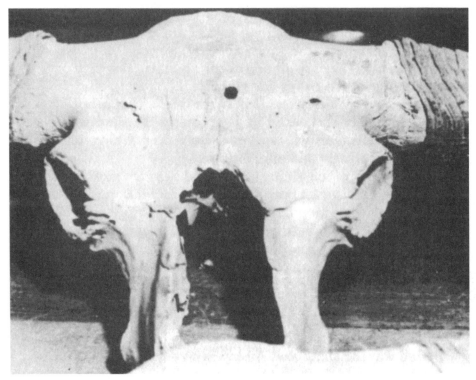

Fig. 36. This skeleton of a bison from the Neolithic can be seen in the Museum of Palaeontology in Moscow. The hole in the skull could only have been made by a fire-arm. Who on earth possessed fire-arms in 8000 B.C.?

museum friends, Chiang, Lynn, Wang and Wu.

These gentlemen's names are supposed to be as common as Smith, Jones and Brown. I tried hard to identify all the happy smiling faces, but I could not manage to put the right name to them.

While I was flying to the Pacific island of Guam by TWA, I drew up a balance of my visit. I had not been able to see the report on Baian Kara Ula, but I had been able to eliminate a white spot on my map of the abodes of the gods on Chinese territory.

Fig. 37. On the night before my departure from Taipeh President Ku Cheng-Kang gave a dinner for me attended by scholars, politicians and museum directors. They all helped my enquiries.

PS.: My film *Chariots of the Gods?* has been bought by Comrade Mao's State Film Lending Library. Perhaps he will help me to make a study trip to Peking. With a post-card in my hand, I'll easily find my way to the Academy with the historical archives.

Besides I have been wanting to visit the Gobi Desert for a long time.

4: *Temuen, the Island they call Nan Madol*

The Caroline Islands form the largest archipelago in Micronesia; there are more than 500 of them, with a total area of 617 sq. miles.

With its 183 sq. miles, Ponape is the biggest of the Caroline Islands, three times as big as the Principality of Liechtenstein and with roughly the same population of 18,000 inhabitants. The climate is tropical and most of the island is mountainous and uninhabitable. Ponape is surrounded by a girdle of other islands, islets and coral reefs. One of the tiny islands, about as big as the Vatican City, is called Temuen, according to the atlas. Temuen is the site of the mighty ruins of Nan Madol, which occupy nearly the whole of the island and account for its importance and fame, so that Temuen has long been known colloquially as Nan Madol. The ruins of Nan Madol go back to the remote past; but its prehistoric layout has not been dated and the origin of its builders is unknown.

These are the historically established dates concerning the island of Ponape and its satellite islets:

1595   Pedro Fernandes de Quiros, a Portuguese, landed from the *San Geronimo*. The first white men set foot on the island and saw the ruins of Nan Madol.

1686   The whole archipelago became a Spanish possession and was called Carolinas after King Charles II.

1826   The Irishman James O'Connell landed on the island with other survivors of a shipwreck. He was given a friendly reception by the people of Ponape and married a native girl.

1838   As from this year, the island's annals record several visits by white men.

1851   Natives massacred the crew of a British ship. A punitive expedition turned Ponape into a bloodbath.

1880   Missionaries of various Christian persuasions descended on the island like a swarm of locusts, burnt age-old inscribed tablets and banned traditional popular customs.

1889   Spain sold the archipelago of Ponape (together with the Marianne and Palau islands) to Germany.

1910   The islanders killed missionaries and government officials. Very few white people escaped the massacre.

1911   The German cruiser *Emden* shelled the island; the rebels were subdued and their leader publicly hanged.

1919   The Caroline Islands, including Ponape, became Japanese mandated territory.

1944   The Americans occupied the group of Islands during the war in the Pacific.

1947   The Islands became American Trust Territory.

Those are the undisputed historical data about Ponape. In other words, it is clear that the mysterious ruins on Nan Madol existed long long before the first visit by white men in 1595. It is not true that the history of the islanders only began to form part of the legend of Nan Madol after they themselves were discovered. Their history since 1595 is more or less completely documented, but the legends about Nan Madol have far more to tell us than these recent facts, which implies that they are infinitely older. Are scholars trying to blind us with science simply because they cannot offer any convincing explanation of the mystery of Nan Madol?

After I had spent over a week in the hot humid hell of
Nan Madol with measuring tape, cameras and notebook,
I can only give a tired smile when I read the previous
'explanations'. I prefer to stick to the legends, because
their contents are more plausible.

We shall see why.

When I landed on Ponape in a Continental Airlines
–Air Micronesia Boeing 727, I had no idea what hard
work my curiosity would let me in for, but neither did I
guess what surprises were in store for me.

The Hotel Kasehlia helped me to charter a small
motorboat, no bigger than a native canoe, and in it I
chugged through the overgrown canals that separated
the many islands from each other. It was oppressively
hot and the air was so humid that I could hardly breathe.
(Fig. 38.)

With my two native guides, I passed several islets and

Fig. 38. One travels between the islets on jungle canals, a world inhabited solely by exotic birds and tropical plants.

then Nan Madol lay ahead of us, looking exactly the same as all the others, except for the strange burden it bore. This tropical island is the site of the small basalt city, the pantheon and legendary retreat of the pre-historic inhabitants, which is no bigger than a football stadium. These evidences of prehistory confront one abruptly; there is no preparation for the 'encounter'.

The ground-plan of the lay-out is clearly recognisable amid the confusion of the ruins, once you have had a good look round. Countless staves are piled on top of each other as in the game of spillikins. It cannot have been an easy game, for the staves are basalt slabs or blocks weighing tons. Until now scholars have claimed that these basalt slabs were formed by lava that had cooled. That seemed a lot of nonsense to me as I labo-riously verified with my measuring-tape that the lava had solidified exclusively in hexagonal or octagonal columns of roughly the same length. (Colour plates 8 and 9.)

As basalt columns actually were extracted on the north coast of Ponape, I am prepared to look beyond the inane explanation of lava columns solidified in uniform sizes and admit that this first-class, accurately worked building material was quarried and dressed on the north coast. So far, so bad, for the blocks, which vary in length from 10 to 29 ft. and often weigh more than 10 tons, must have been transported from the north coast of Ponape all the way through the labyrinth of jungle canals, past dozens of equally serviceable islands, to Nan Madol. Transport by land is excluded, because since the re-motest times downpours have flooded the dense jungle several times a day and in addition Ponape is mountain-ous. Even if we assume that roads were hacked out of the jungle and that there were means of transport that could surmount the mountains and force a way through the marshy morasses, the heavy loads would still only have reached the south-east corner of the island and would then have had to be loaded on to ships.

I was told by locals that the transport problem could easily have been solved by using rafts. This explanation contradicts another one which a scholar seriously tried to 'sell' me, namely that the original inhabitants suspended the basalt blocks from their canoes, thus reducing the weight, and rowed them to Nan Madol one by one.

I took the trouble to count the basalt blocks in one side of the main building. I counted 1,082 columns on a façade 195 ft. long. The building is square and the four outside walls contain 4,782 basalt blocks. I got a mathematician to calculate the volume of the walls from their breadth and height and the number of basalt columns necessary to fill it. The main building 'swallowed up' about 32,000. Yet the main building is only part of the layout. See map (fig. 39).

There are canals, ditches, tunnels and an 875-yard-long wall, which measures 46 ft. 6 ins. at its highest point. The rectangular main precinct is arranged in terraces which are also built of perfect basalt squares. The main house that I measured has more than 80 outbuildings. Using the figure of 32,000 as a basis, an estimate of about 4,000,000 basalt columns installed in the 80 minor buildings alone is probably on the low side. A trial calculation is often enough to show up false explanations. Like this one, for example:

At the time when the complex of buildings on Nan Madol was constructed there was a small number of inhabitants on Ponape compared with today. The quarrying work on the north coast was difficult, laborious and boring. Transporting the dressed blocks through the jungle needed a whole army of strong men, and the number of dock labourers who tied the blocks under the canoes was also considerable. Lastly a number of islanders must have been engaged in harvesting the

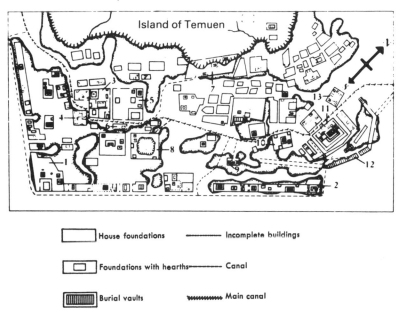

Fig. 39. This ground-plan of the buildings at Nan Madol was made by Paul Hambruch during his field-work in 1908–1910. It was brought up to date by K. Masao Hadley. The foundations are clearly visible among the ruins.

coconut palms, fishing and looking after the daily supply of food. Thus, if every fourth day several tons of basalt blocks reached the south coast for onward transport to Nan Madol, it would have been a gigantic, remarkable achievement, with the 'technical' aids available. As there can have been no trade unions in those days, I assume that everybody worked and slaved 365 days a year. If 1,460 basalt blocks a year were landed on Nan Madol, it would have taken 296 years merely to get the material to the building site!

No, human beings have never been so stupid as to submit to such torture pointlessly. If there were basalt quarries on the north coast of Ponape, *why* didn't they erect the group of buildings on the main island? *Why* did they build on an islet so far away from the quarry?

Is there no convincing explanation?

Nan Madol is by no means a 'beautiful' city and it obviously never was. There are no reliefs, no sculptures, no statues or paintings. The architecture is cold and unfriendly. The basalt blocks are piled on top of each other harshly, crudely, threateningly. This is surprising because the South Sea islanders always decorated their palaces and fortresses lavishly. Palaces and fortresses were places in which kings were to be honoured.or the gods appeased. The Spartan masonry of Nan Madol excludes either of these alternatives. Was it a defence work? The terraces that facilitate the climb up to the buildings reduce that supposition *ad absurdum*. No one ever made things so easy for their enemies. In fact, the terraces lead to the centre of the plan, to the 'well'.

This well is not a well, but the way down to the beginning or end of a tunnel. The fact that today the opening is full of water to barely six feet below the edge proves nothing, for the buildings of Nan Madol continue over the edge of the island and can be followed with the naked eye below sea level until they disappear in the depths.

But what was a tunnel doing on a tiny island? Where did it lead?

I first read about this remarkable feature in Herbert Rittlinger's book *The Measureless Ocean*. Rittlinger, who travelled round the South Seas on a voyage of research, learnt on Ponape that the brilliant and splendid centre of a celebrated kingdom had existed there untold millennia ago. The reports of fabulous wealth had enticed pearl divers and Chinese merchants to investigate the seabed secretly and the divers had all risen from the depths with incredible tales. They had been able to walk on the bottom on well-preserved streets overgrown with mussels and coral. 'Down below', there were countless stone vaults, pillars and monoliths. Carved stone tablets hung on the remains of clearly recognisable houses.

What the pearl divers did not find was discovered by Japanese divers with modern equipment. They confirmed with their finds what the traditional legends of Ponape reported: the vast wealth in precious metals, pearls and bars of silver. The legend says that the corpses rest in the 'House of the Dead' (i.e. the main house in the complex). The Japanese divers reported that the dead were buried in watertight platinum coffins. And the divers actually brought bits of platinum to the surface day after day! In fact, the main exports of the island —copra, vanilla, sago and mother of pearl—were supplanted by platinum! Rittlinger says that the Japanese carried on exploiting this platinum until one day two divers did not surface, in spite of their modern equipment. Then the war broke out and the Japanese had to withdraw. He ends his story as follows:

'The natives' stories, encrusted with century-old legends, are probably exaggerated. But the finds of platinum on an island where the rock contains no platinum, were and remain a very real fact.'

All that happened about 1939.

I do not believe in the metal or platinum coffins. Hexagonal or octagonal basalt columns, overgrown with mussels and coral, could easily be mistaken for coffins under the water. Never mind. The fact remains that Japan exported platinum from Ponape after its mandate in 1919.

Where did all this platinum come from?

Even if the coffins were an illusion, I am convinced by the divers' tales of houses, streets and stone vaults on the sea bottom, for one can see these structures in clear water at the edge of the island and recognise clearly how they lead to the so-called well. In my opinion, this was most probably the entrance to a tunnel system covering the island. One point: Nan Madol has nothing in common with the legendary Atlantis that vanished into the sea in 9000 B.C., according to Plato. Here the buildings on dry land exist on the spot where they were laid out ages ago and their continuations under water were planned layouts which were constructed at the same time. There are relics of wonderful buildings here, but there is no miracle.

What does tradition say about the mysterious ruins of Nan Madol?

K. Masao Hadley, Pensile Lawrence and Carole Jencks, research workers living on Ponape, have collected material without attempting to interpret it.

The main building is referred to as the 'Temple of the Holy Dove' in the legend. Only three centuries ago, Nanususunsap, the Dove God and high priest, was rowed through the canals in a boat and opposite him sat a dove which he had to look in the eyes all the time. If the dove blinked—and doves do so constantly—the poor high priest had to blink back. A strange conceit.

However, the legends relate that originally the symbol of Nan Madol was not a dove, but a fire-breathing dragon. The stories about the origin of the island and the buildings are woven round this formerly indigenous dragon. The dragon's mother had excavated the canals with her powerful muzzle and so created the islets. The dragon had a magician as helper and this dragon-magician knew a rhyme with which, thanks to the power of the charm, he could make the basalt blocks fly over from the neighbouring island, and then, with the help of another rhyme, use them to make buildings without the inhabitants of Nan Madol lifting a finger.

I was amused by one interpretation of the dragon legend. The archaeologists say that the dragon was not really a dragon, but a crocodile that made its way to Nan Madol by mistake and created a considerable disturbance there. There are crocodiles in the South Seas about 3,000 miles from the island. A crocodile might have lost its way at some time—why not?—but that would still not be a reason for bringing a solitary saurian into the legend and leaving out the actual building of the edifices at Nan Madol, which is far more impressive. *One* crocodile left traces behind in the popular legend, but buildings whose elements are still astonishing and inexplicable today are left unmentioned. The crocodile obviously did not build terraces, houses and tunnels. Or did it?

Naturally there are many more legends about Nan Madol than those of the dove and dragon. In the second volume of his *Results of the South Sea Expedition, 1908–1910* (Berlin, 1936), the German ethnologist Paul Hambruch gives a detailed survey of the sagas, myths and legends of the Caroline Islands. The District Economic Development Office on Ponape sells tourists a brochure containing data about the history and legends for a dollar. If I have concentrated here on the dragon legend, I have a good reason for doing so. It is not because I have found a *unique* key witness for my theory of the gods.

On all the South Sea islands which can show the ruins of ancient buildings and confirm their past in myths, one finds the wild claim that big stones flew through the air to their appointed places. The most prominent of these legends-cum-prophecies (because it is world-famous) concerns Easter Island. In their myths the Rapanui have handed down through the ages the 'knowledge' that some 200 colossal statues around the coast of the island landed in their positions 'from the air' and 'by themselves'.

The dragon and dove legends are found everywhere, naturally in different versions. The mass of additional legendary material is dominated by warlike events, lists of the descendants of ruling royal families, marriages and murders, as well as verifiable historical facts of more recent date. This extensive part of the legends is based on facts; it has a core of reality. That seems only logical to me, for even the boldest imagination needs a spur, a launching pad, as it were, for daring ideas. Thus, when it is dealing with an apparent Utopia, the human imagination tends to use what it has experienced or at least what is conceivable at that time. Now dragons are a global element in myths and legends. The earliest Chinese sagas mention them and they have their natural place in Mayan mythology. These fire-breathing monsters are familiar to every ancient people in the South Sea community, though sometimes in the form of noisy, flying snakes. But they all possess the fabulous art of being able to carry very large and heavy objects over vast distances and setting them up in a prearranged order in a given place. What master builder of our own day would not like to be a dragon with such abilities?

The imaginative early inhabitants built Nan Madol. Not in a day. With the help of a friendly mathematician, I calculated that it would have taken them about 300 years. They toiled with blood, sweat and tears for many generations. Why has not this tremendous achievement by the islanders been recorded and given prominence in *established* history if—as the archaeologists claim—it only took place 500 years ago? The 'proof' of this recent dating is very flimsy. Six years ago some charcoal remains were found under a basalt block near the 'well'. Carbon 14 examination gave a date around A.D. 1300.

Apart from the well-attested inaccuracy of the C 14 method, which presupposes a constant relation of the radioactive isotope of carbon (C) with the atomic weight 14 in the atmosphere, it is much more possible or even probable that later generations lit a fire on the basalt buildings that had already been in existence for a long time. These are not proofs to be taken seriously, they are tricks to bluff us when scholars have nothing else to rely on.

Polynesia (Greek: country of many islands), the archipelago of the eastern ocean, lies in the large triangle between Hawaii, Easter Island and New Zealand. The original inhabitants of all the Polynesian islands (total area 15,800 sq. miles) have common sagas and legends; they have common linguistic roots and with only a few variations they have a common appearance. They also have common gods!

The majority of Polynesian specialists—archaeologists, anthropologists and philologists—are united in saying that culture and language spread from East Polynesia. According to this version, the export of culture spread from the group of the nine Cook Islands and their many atolls, from the large island of Tahiti (387 sq. miles), from the Tuamoto Islands, with approximately 80 atolls, and from the Marquesas and the Mangareva Islands.

I dare not belittle these scientific conclusions, but I have some questions to ask.

How did the East Polynesians cover the vast distance between the islands when they were carrying on their export trade in culture?

There is a theory that they boarded their canoes, rowed into the ocean currents and then drifted. Where did they drift to?

It is half a century since research into marine currents has given us a pretty accurate idea of the directions in which the large strong currents move and which coasts they touch. The map of marine currents shows conclusively that the East Polynesian exporters must have reached New Zealand, the biggest island in the South Pacific, in their primitive canoes *against* the current.

A favourite explanation of this motorless and compassless traffic is that the seafarers between East Polynesia and New Zealand travelled so far in a northerly or southerly direction that they found themselves east or west of their goal—then the clever fellows slipped into the currents at exactly the right place.

That would be all right if the ancient Polynesians had had modern maritime knowledge and navigational aids. What did they know about the precise degree of latitude from which they had to turn off to east or west? And how did they know their goal? Did they know that other islands existed and where they were?

Anyone who assumes that the ancient Polynesians made exact use of the currents—that ran counter to the directions of their expeditions—must be prepared to admit that knowledge of marine currents was familiar to them. If scholars are ready to admit this necessary prerequisite for navigation between the islands, I will gladly support the current theory, but at the same time I must be allowed to ask the question *whence* they acquired this knowledge.

We are concerned here with the export of culture from east to west over vast distances, which I list here according to data supplied by international airlines:

Easter Island–Tahiti	= 2,300 miles
Tahiti–Fiji	= 2,670 miles
Fiji–Australia	= 1,865 miles
California–Hawaii	= 2,485 miles
Hawaii–Marshall Islands	= 2,360 miles

But if in spite of this, a raft or a canoe had landed by chance on the coast of a hitherto unknown island, the bold seafarers (against the current!) would never again have had any communication with their former home; they could not even have sent messages saying that they had landed. If the foolhardy aquanauts had happened to put to sea again from the island they had landed on by chance, they would have got further and further away from their home port. Not even the strongest men could have managed the journey home in canoes. Yet according to science they had another astounding achievement to their credit. They had no women with them, but they not only supplied the islands with culture, but also produced children who then multiplied vigorously. How did they manage that?

The East Polynesians navigated by the stars! 'If the Southern Cross is on the horizon at midnight, we must steer to the left to reach Bora-Bora.'

How did the culture-bearers know where Bora-Bora lay? Had someone been on the many hundred islands before them? In what way did the 'discoverers' receive from their home island the reports that were necessary for fixing their positions?

Today the seaman *knows* that his goal exists (unlike the prehistoric discoverer); he knows where it lies and on what route it is to be found. The original Polynesians lacked all the necessary knowledge. If they reached an island, a lucky chance had put it in their way.

The intelligent and skilful inhabitants of New Zealand, the Maoris, have a saga which gives cause for reflection.

It tells us that in early times there was a King Kupe, who undertook what was obviously a kind of scientific expedition in company with his two daughters and two birds. Kupe discovered the East Coast of New Zealand, went ashore and sent the two birds off to reconnoitre. One bird was given the task of measuring the marine currents and the drop in the rivers, the other had to analyse berries and plants to see if they were edible. The first bird broke its wings while measuring a waterfall and being lame could no longer fly. The second bird, so the Maori saga goes, discovered such a delicious kind of berry that it decided to spend the rest of its life in the forest. Kupe never saw it again. Consequently, it continues, King Kupe and his daughters could not return home.

Why couldn't they?

The king still had the canoe with which he began the expedition. Both daughters, presumably athletic young ladies, were with him. In spite of this, the journey home was impossible. Did he use the clever birds, which could do far more than just fly according to the saga, for navigation?

The remarkable nature of this tale is far exceeded in the oldest Maori legend, which claims that New Zealand was fished from the waters of the deep by the god Maaui!

The legend relates that Maaui hooked a fish that fought and bit and snapped so wildly that the god got into a rage and cut and hacked the fish to bits . . . and that is why New Zealand is in pieces the way it is.

Today the Maoris still call the North Island Te Ika-A-Maaui, the fish of Maaui, after the traditional legend of their forefathers, while the South Island (Stewart Island) is the god's boat to them. The Mahia peninsula, Te Matau a Maaui, is the fish-hook, the Wellington region, Te Upoko O Te Ika, the head, and the North Auckland peninsula, Te Hiku O Te Ika, the fish's tail.

That is a story that bears thinking about. When the god Maaui caught land, there were no maps in existence. But one look at the atlas confirms how accurately this legend outlines the shapes of New Zealand. You can see the ray-like fish with its open mouth in the south, and the long tail in the north with one fin on the hook.

From time immemorial the Polynesians have been fishermen themselves, they have caught the 'fruits of the sea' of all kinds on hooks or in nets, and probably like fishermen everywhere they told tall stories about their catches. But they always knew that it was impossible to angle or fish for *land*. Nevertheless, legends on all the islands claim that the god Maaui was the 'fisher of land'.

With a touch of our magic wand let us turn the god Maaui into that valiant aviator Charles Lindbergh who flew the 3,750 miles from New York to Paris in 33 hours on 20 and 21 May, 1927. Alone in the windlashed, one-engined machine, all he could see below him was water, water, water. One and a half days all alone high above the water—a nightmare! Way down below Lindbergh saw a dark spot. A big fish? An island? A shoal of fish? An archipelago? Lindbergh slowly reduced altitude until he recognised that the dark spot in the Atlantic consisted of islands. The lone aviator's tension relaxed; he had 'fished' a bit of land. Very funny, I shall be told, because the Polynesians in the remote past had not mastered the art of flying.

I am convinced with a probability bordering on certainty that the earliest Polynesians could fly.

The objects catalogued as masks (fig. 40) will easily be recognised as poor copies of one-man flying machines by anyone who does not obstinately claim in the face of all prehistoric evidence that they are 'religious masks', 'ritual garments' or 'ritual requisites' (whichever suits the anthropologists best) and who is also prepared to interpret the finds on Polynesian islands (and elsewhere) from the modern point of view. The 'masks' were pulled over the head from above; the movable flat wooden side pieces were nothing more or less than wings. One can see the holes for fitting the arms through at the other end. Even the arm and leg supports, yes, the whole 'corset' into which the aviator had to squeeze himself, have remained a memory to Polynesian folk artists for millennia. Obviously they no longer know why they decorate and equip their gods and kings with such complicated apparatuses. No one has been able to *fly* with this gear for many many thousands of years. But in the remote

Fig. 40. The Bishop Museum at Honolulu, Hawaii, contains many such copies of flying machines, catalogued as 'ritual masks' by scholars. But it would take less imagination to identify these 'memories', which have been made for many centuries, as aids to flying that were pulled over the head, with the flat pieces of wood as wings, with supports for arms and legs and the corset into which the flyer had to squeeze himself.

There is a massive gold sphere in the cosmological treasure chamber of Maria Auxiliadora at Cuenca, Ecuador. The broad flange could equally well be a docking ramp for suppply ships and a storeroom, divided into cells, for solar energy. The technical possibilities we can imagine are endless. The negative in stone is in the Turkish Museum in Istanbul.

Father Carlo Crespi, who collected and guarded an incredible treasure of gold and silver objects in the back patio of the Church of Maria Auxiliadora at Cuenca.

The dominant feature of this gold plaque is a pyramid on which snakes writhe upwards. Do the circles indicate the number of astronauts buried inside it?

A heavy gold discus, 8-1/2 inches in diameter. A precious and mysterious means of conveying information, but certainly not a normal shield!

Notable features of this solid gold pyramid: the snakes are where they belong—in the sky—and at its foot are elephants, which the artists could not possibly have seen in South America in the past. The writing on the lower edge of the pyramid is unknown and has not been deciphered so far.

This gold figure, 20 inches high, has normal human proportions, but only four fingers and four toes on hands and feet. The serioius scienticfic explanation? An adding machine (for the number four)! Were the early South Americans so stupid as to make a whole figure just to represent a "four"? Really, this is the "Star God"—an extraterrestrial.

One keeps on making new discovereies on this gold plaque, which measures 38-1/2 inches by 19 inches by 1 inch. A star, a being with a fat paunch, a man in a coat of mail with a helmet, faces, a wheel with a face peeping out of it, a face with another one growing out of it and and and ... The whole chaotic scene is menaced by a **falling bomb**, which the artist empasized by placing it between two hinges.

Above: These balls lie in Moeraki Bay, New Zealand, as if they had risen from the sea. Unlike the similar phenomenon in Costa Rica, these balls originated from natural causes—135,000,000 years ago in the Upper Cretaceous.

Opposite page: The basalt slabs of Nan Madol, which are piled up to a height of 80 feet in some places, are hexagonal or octagonal and as much as 16 feet long. More than 80 outbuildings, arranged on artifical terraces, surround the main building. The whole is enclosed by a protective walll 937 yards long and 16 feet high.

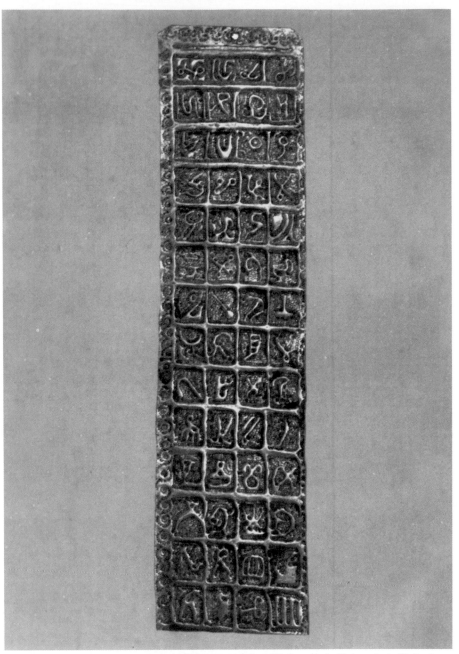

This gold stele is the show pice. It is 20-1/2 by 5-1/2 by 1-1/2 inches. 56 different characters are "stamped" on its 56 squares. The folios of the metal library in the Great Hall have exaclty the same signs! Did the maker of this stele know a code, an alphabet with 56 signs or symbols, which were arranged to form writing? Until now it has been claimed that there were no scripts using alphabets in the South American cultures.

times when Maaui 'fished' the islands, certain specialists among the population *could* fly with these machines!

In the Bishop Museum in Honolulu, which houses the biggest Polynesian collection in the world, several long passages are full of these flying machines. Large numbers of similar machines are stored in the Museum in Auckland. These admittedly poor copies of very early flying machines have been promptly and without exception declared 'ritual attributes' on all sites and in all museums.

The four-winged beings in Assyria were ritual beings. Pottery artefacts with technical drawings of circular and spherical ornaments were ritual objects.

The technical-looking objects in the hands of the statues of Tula were ritual objects.

The space traveller on the tombstone at Palenque was an Indian in a ritual pose.

The clearly recognisable packs and tubes (supply systems) on the backs of Mayan priests were ritual accoutrements.

And naturally the fibre frames on the Polynesian islands were also turned into ritual masks.

Such stupidity reminds me of the title of a novel by Mosheh Y. Ben-Gavriel, *Camels Drink from Dry Wells, too.*

The Polynesians did not discover the key to the art of flying on their own. They had teachers, who spent some time on earth in ages unknown to us. Since they came from an extremely advanced civilisation, I assume that technical trifles were a spare-time hobby for them and that one of their inventions was the rocket-belt. (Fig. 41.) Americans and Russians use these one-man flying machines, originally constructed for space travel, to take individual commandos to their destination over hills and rivers. Even one-man helicopters are no longer a Utopian idea. Rotor blades are mounted on a motor carried on the back; on the chest is a small box with the controls.

If a child was given some wood and straw and asked to knock up a strange aviator like those that he had seen on television, a 'ritual mask' would certainly result. But the child would consider it as 'his' flyer.

Now it would clearly be exceeding the ration of audacity I have allowed myself if I were to claim that the earliest ancestors of the Polynesians had teachers from an alien technologically advanced civilisation from the cosmos . . . if the South Seas' peoples legends did not do precisely that.

In his *Ancient History of the Maori,* New Zealand, 1887, John White has assembled South Sea legends with the scrupulous care of a scholar. When he began his work in 1880, he was told many prehistoric stories at first hand by the priests. The subjects in the first volume alone show where the origin of prehistory is to be sought:

The gods' family tree
The story of the creation
War in the universe
The creation of man and woman
The Flood and stories about the Ark
Marriages between gods and men
Journeys between the earth and other stars
Food that fell from heaven.

The Rongamai legend is about tribal warfare. Afraid of being overcome, the Nga-Ti-Hau tribe sought safety in a fortified village. When they were threatened by an invincible opponent even there, the Nga-Ti-Hau warriors sought the help of the god Rongamai. When the sun was at its zenith, the god appeared:

'His appearance was
like a shining star,
like a fiery flame,
like a sun.'

Fig. 41. The contemporary counterpart to the South Sea Islanders' flying machine: rocket belts as used by Americans and Russians for one-man commandos. Yet archaeologists would say that when our children make imitation rocket belts of wood and straw they are making ritual masks!

Rongamai flew over the village square and landed:

'The ground was stirred up,
Clouds of dust blocked our gaze,
The noise rolled like thunder,
Then like the rushing sound in a mussel shell.'

The warriors were given fresh courage by this display of strength by the god and overran their astounded enemies.

In the Tawhaki legend the maiden Hapai descends from the seventh heaven to earth to spend the nights there with a 'handsome man'. This chosen man knows nothing of the maiden's origin; not until she is pregnant does she reveal the 'truth' that she came from a distant world beyond his ken where she held the rank of goddess. Then, no longer a maiden, she brings a daughter into the world and after giving birth returns into the cosmos.

The multiplicity of aids with which the mystery-enshrouded deities return to the universe is bewildering. Sometimes endless ladders are used, which then disappear and are never seen again, sometimes towers are present to aid the start, sometimes spiders' webs or vine tendrils are strong enough to set the travellers moving heavenwards, but they are also often carried by birds or dragons, or enter the void on ropes. But whatever the variant an old woman is always present at take off. Crouching on the ground, she counts potatoes. She warns the deities of 'winds that blow earthwards' and then she throws the potatoes into the fire, one after another, nine, eight, seven, six, five . . . The old woman organised a regular countdown, just like they do at a Space Centre.

In *Polynesian Mythology*, Wellington, New Zealand

(undated), there is a legend which the Polynesian fishermen used to tell:

'The warrior Uenuku was walking along the shore by the sea when he saw a column of mist floating in the air above the beach. He summoned up his courage and approached the apparition. He saw two wondrous fair maidens who had descended from heaven to bathe in the sea. Driven by an irresistible force he went up to the maidens and greeted them respectfully. Delighted by the sight, he asked one of them to accompany him to his house and be his wife.
The fair one answered:
"I love this world.
It is not cold and empty
like the lofty space up there." '

It is remarkable that the simple Polynesian fishermen should mention a cold, empty, lofty space 'up there' in their legend. They knew a lot about land and sea, but how did they know about the lofty space up there?
The same source supplies a really grotesque legendary account:
Rupe, who also appears under the name of Maui Mua, set forth to seek his sister Hinaura. As he could not find her, he sought the advice of his ancestor Rehua, who lived in heaven in a place called Te Putahi Hui O Rehua.
Rupe girded and masked himself and climbed up to the heaven.
He reached a place where men lived and asked:
'Are the heavens above this heaven inhabited?'
'Yes, they are inhabited,' he was told.
'Can I reach these heavens?'
'No, you will never be able to reach them for these heavens were built by Tane.'

Rupe struggled up to the second heaven and again found men, whom he also asked:

'Are the heavens above these heavens inhabited?'

'Yes, but you will never be able to reach them because they were built by Tane.'

Yet again Rupe struggled upwards and again he found a place that was inhabited.

'Are the heavens above these heavens inhabited?'

'Yes, but you will never reach them, for your *mask* is not by Tane.'

Rupe did not give up, laboriously and with his last remaining strength he reached the tenth heaven where he found Rehua (also known as Hinaura).

The Ancient History of the Maori tells us that this almighty Tane was the god of the forests and animals. One legend recounts that he created the first woman and another that after the *second great war in the heavens* Tane forced the rebel gods to descend to *other worlds in the darkness to live there in despair for eternity.* But Tane supplied the losers of the cosmic battle with all his knowledge and skills for their flight into damnation.

Is it necessary to explain this perfectly clear text any further? Need I point out that apparatuses and masks were necessary for a flight in the universe? Do I have to tell a generation that watched all stages of the moon flight live on television that one heaven after another has to be conquered? And that to do this tremendous know-how is essential, whether NASA or Tane is involved.

I should also like to remind readers of the main work of the Cabbala, the Book Zohar, which contains Rabbi Simon Bar Jochai's report of a conversation between an earth-dweller and a being stranded from the world of Arqua. Refugees, who had survived a terrestrial catastrophe, were walking along led by Rabbi Yossé when they met a stranger who suddenly emerged from a

crack in the rock. Yossé asked the stranger where he
came from. He answered:

'I am an inhabitant of Arqua.'

The surprised Rabbi asked:

'You mean that there are living creatures on Arqua?'

The stranger replied:

'Yes. When I saw you coming, I climbed out of the
hole to find out the name of the world on which I had
landed.'

And he said that in 'his' world the seasons were different from those in 'their' land, that there seed and harvest
would only renew themselves after several years and that
the inhabitants of Arqua *visited all worlds and spoke all languages*.

The Cabbala mentions seven different worlds, but it
also says that only Arqua sent emissaries to earth.

These direct and unequivocal references to other
worlds (other planets) are there in the legends. I cannot
change them. They are always interpreted with the old
exegeses that have led nowhere. Yes, say the exegetes,
such legends cannot be explained unless one adopts the
way of thinking of our remote ancestors. But do they do
that? They *think* they do. In reality the conceptual world
of prehistoric peoples, some of whom have vanished
without trace, simply cannot be recreated in retrospect,
we can only guess that they *must* have thought in such
and such a way. It is only an assumption. Every interpretation is ensnared and caught in the way of thinking of
the age in which it is made, but even then with limita-
tions.

The blinkers come down as soon as subjective explanations based on the knowledge available in this space age
are attempted. They are not allowed.

Because there is no flying in prehistory, there cannot
have been any contact with other planets. Full stop. But
how do people try to extricate themselves from the

morass of the inexplicable? They turn to psychology. The legends were wishful thinking on the part of the unconscious. They even enrol my fellow-countryman Carl Gustav Jung (1875–1961) with his doctrine of psychic energy, his theory of individuation, and especially his theory of the archetype with primordial innate ways of behaviour and images. The world is in order again. 'Man has always wanted to be able to fly like a bird.' Innate ways of behaviour? Primordial images? I have nothing against the wish to be able to fly, I like flying very much myself. Does that mean that our early ancestors had the same longing? Did the unconscious supply them with absolutely realistic mental images of flying machines; did it give them accurate data about worlds that they had never seen? Did it guide their hand when they sketched technical details in cave paintings? Or when they carved integrated circuits on the Gate of the Sun at Tiahuanaco?

In the Babylonian epic Etana is obsessed with the wish to fly. He may have dreamt about it, he may have talked about it, but neither dreams nor imagination can have given him such a picturesque description of the earth's surface as the one in the epic:

'The earth was like a garden
and the sea furrowed into the land
like the trenches dug by a gardener.'

And wishful thinking could not possibly have supplied Enkidu with the description of the earth—as seen from above—in the Epic of Gilgamesh.

'And the land was like a mountain and the sea like a small puddle . . . And the land looked like porridge and the sea like a water trough.'

In Volume 18 of the *Yearbook of the Society of German Engineers*, Berlin, 1928, Professor Richard Henning examines texts relevant to the prehistory of air travel. He describes the Etana legend as definitely the 'oldest flying saga in the world', and one which must go back to the very beginning of history, because it is already represented *pictorially* on a cylinder seal from the period between 3000 and 2400 B.C., whereas the text has been only partially preserved in a cuneiform inscription. This passage struck the professor as especially noteworthy:

> 'Not on the eagle's back, but clamped breast to breast with it was Etana carried up to the heaven of the fixed stars . . . Six times during the upward flight the eagle drew Etana's attention to the earth which was growing smaller and smaller before their eyes.'

Accurate descriptions, pictorial representations as products of the unconscious? Here I think the psychoanalysts should curb the adepts of their science if they themselves want to remain credible.

Our research into myths and legends and the interpretations of archaeology are—as far as they concern prehistory—tied up in a straitjacket of preconceived views. Eyes have grown blind, ideas become dead. Science says that it cannot accept imaginative solutions because they have no empirical or demonstrable foundation. But now serious conclusions become more and more fantastic every day, while at the same time the disparaged fantasies acquire a firmer background. Three premises are the basis of all research: freedom of thought, a gift for observation and a sense of connections. Laymen can make use of them too.

Let us fly back to the South Seas again!

There Maori legends are haunted by the god Pourangahua (fig. 42), who flew from his legendary seat of

Hawaiki to New Zealand on a magic bird. Hawaiki is a compound word that comes from Old Indian and can be translated as 'from the Milky Way'. The oldest Maori prayer is attributed to this Pourangahua:

'I come,
and an unknown earth
lies below my feet.
I come

Fig. 42. According to the Maori legend, the god Pourangahua flew on his magic bird from his legendary dwelling Hawaiki to New Zealand. 'I come and a new heaven turns above me. . .'

and a new heaven turns above me.
I come
on to this earth and it is
a peaceful resting-place for me.
O spirit of the planets!
The stranger humbly offers you
his heart as nourishment.'

On the beaches and roadsides visitors to New Zealand see large round balls with diameters up to 10 ft. 5 ins. On Moeraki Beach, north of Dunedin, dozens of them of all sizes are strewn about (colour plate 10). Having become interested in balls after seeing the *artificial* stone balls of Costa Rica, I naturally examined the New Zealand variety very closely. *These* balls originated from *natural* causes. They form in soft sandstone by deposits of calc-spar around a core. Geologists date the beginning of the formation of the balls to the Upper Cretaceous, 135,000,000 years ago. Although they are of natural origin, there are some strange varieties among them, the so-called geodes.

A geode is a word used in geology that comes from the Greek. It consists of a stone in which a hollow space has been caused by gas, the space being wholly or partially filled with minerals or crystalline deposits. Geodes are not only eagerly sought after by geologists, but also by businesslike laymen who turn them into desirable trinkets for sale in gift shops by cutting, halving, quartering and polishing them. Treasure seekers of this kind found a stone that looked like a geode in 1961 near Olancha, on the edge of the Amargosa Desert. So they put it in their collecting basket, the contents of which they prepared for sale on their return. When they tried to saw through the putative geode, the diamond saw broke, because the stone was not hollow, but solid, in spite of its appearance. Geologists who dissected the stone found inside it

an unknown stone with an iridescent surface that had
been formed under the effect of intense heat. In its core
was a shining metal rod 2 mm. in diameter and 17 mm.
long.

Strange?

'There are more things in heaven and earth, Horatio,
Than are dreamt on in your philosophy.'

The American Trust Administration is doing its best
to improve the infrastructure of the island. Roads are
being built on Ponape; an electricity works is already
functioning; the harbour is being enlarged; a radio station floods the island and its islets with music. But this is
all in its early stages, which makes it all the more surprising that nearly every native family on the impoverished
island is the proud possessor of a car! In many huts, even
those without electricity, there are juke-boxes. The
owner of my so-called first-class hotel had three of them
and they were always nerve-rackingly in use. The few
guests could pass the time playing the two pin-tables and
on the day I left the island an electric adding machine
was delivered to his establishment. I could not find the
secret behind this absurd wealth. The natives are poor
and incurably lazy and have no interest in business. I
had to use all my powers of persuasion even to find two
boys to take me over to Nan Madol every day. Americans
are known to be wonderful salesmen, but they want to
see some money for their goods. Where do the islanders
get all the money for so many useless things? I kept on
remembering the Japanese divers who had brought
pieces of platinum up from the ocean bed.

Perhaps I missed a chance to get to the bottom of all
secrets in one moment of complete clairvoyance.

On the day before my departure, I was invited by some
natives to their village. I had known for a long time that
such gestures of hospitality ought not to be rejected. You

can never return to the village which has invited you, if you have been impolite. The oldest woman of the tribe greeted me and led me through some huts to the village square. Women and girls crouched in front of a hollow tree trunk and when they caught sight of me began to beat out a rhythm with sticks that had a kind of blues tempo. Men and boys entered the circle and began to stamp their feet, and as they gyrated they beat very skilfully on some more tree trunks that gave out a different note. They drew me into their ring, which was quite calm to begin with, but hotted up terribly as the ladies' rhythm group set a fearful tempo. The air was hot and sticky and I had to join in, jumping up and down, running and stamping in the circle—the only thing I was spared was the wooden spear. The rock'n'roll of the fifties was like a tango compared to our performance.

But there was worse to come.

I was led into a hut. There was a large flat stone on the ground and I and six men were placed round it. Teenagers brought the fresh roots of a young tree (Lat. *piper methysticum*). The roots were superficially cleaned with bunches of lianas and laid on the stone. The men took stone pounders and hammered the roots in unison for about half an hour. The roots turned into a sticky brown porridge-like mass. The teenagers brought vegetable fibres and spread them carefully on the edge of the stone. Then the men who had been pounding the roots spread the mixture on the fibres, which were then tied to a rope. The evil sauce that dripped into coconut shells was *sakao*. An innocent youth—the rites prescribe that it must be an innocent youth—knelt before me and proffered me the shell, without looking me in the eyes (which is strictly forbidden). The things one does in the name of international understanding! I raised the shell to my lips; all eyes were on me and I forced down a couple of mouthfuls. I handed the shell to my neighbour who swallowed the fearful brew as if it were vintage champagne. The shell was refilled and everyone enjoyed the festive drinking bout until they soon lay down and fell into a deep blissful sleep.*

Sakao acts like a drug, but is not addictive and does not give you a headache when you wake up. Connoisseurs told me that *sakao* is supposed to have an effect like LSD. I have read that LSD produces moments of unprecedented incredible clairvoyance. If I had swallowed more of the vile juice, I might possibly have been granted that illumination which would have explained the secrets of Nan Madol in a flash. So I shall have to hand on my questions to the experts, who so far have been seeing 'in a glass darkly', with singular lack of clairvoyance.

By the way, Nan Madol is a composite word from the language of the Ponapes and means 'Place of the intermediate spaces'.

* The same drink is called *yangona* in the Fiji Islands and *kava* on Tonga and Samoa.

5: *On the Trail of the Indians*

From the southernmost tip of Sicily to Hammerfest, the most northerly town in Europe, you fly over eight countries in the course of your 2,500-mile journey. Flying from Moscow to the South Yemen, which is about the same distance, you see seven nations below you. But if you fly from Cacipore to the Rio Grande, some 2,500 to 2,700 miles in a north-south direction, there is only one country below you all the time: Brasil. It is just the same in a west-east direction—from the Peruvian border to Recife on the Atlantic Ocean it is all Brasil. With a surface area of 3,289,440 sq. miles, the gigantic South American country is only exceeded in its endless extent by Russia, China, Canada and the USA.

Besides being vast, Brasil is full of mysteries.

If a pilot of the VASP airline on a routine flight of 1,250 miles sees towers or villages or ruins that are not marked on the map, he notes down their geographical position and makes a report. But if someone sets out to verify the data only three days later, the towers, villages or ruins may have already disappeared. What was only briefly visible in favourable weather conditions, when the wind was right or after a forest fire, has already been overgrown, swallowed up again by that green Moloch, the forest.

Brasil is a country of extremes. It is as difficult to get to know its present as it is to get to know its past. Since Dodge, VW, Ford and Chevrolet have been making all kinds of cars here, army pioneers are constantly turning up archaeological finds when building the new roads intended to open up the vast territories which are still

127

inaccessible. No one can estimate how much unique material is lost for ever in the mountains of debris excavated.

Archaeology is a universal hobby in Brasil, but professional archaeologists are rare. If finds as rich as these were made in other countries, universities would initiate research projects or governments provide financial aid for excavation teams under expert leadership. It is quite different here.

The size of the country and the multiplicity of archaeological riches, most of them virtually inaccessible, mean that planned digging, classification and excavation scarcely ever take place. Even if a forgotten prehistoric town is accurately located and accessible with the right kind of vehicle, it takes years before the money to equip a modern expedition is available. Only too often the result is that it comes too late.

Archaeological finds in Brasil are mostly due to the luck, industry and keenness of enthusiastic laymen. The Austrian Ludwig Schwennhagen was one of them. He was a teacher of philosophy and history and lived for a long time in Teresina, the capital of the north Brasilian state of Piaui. Schwennhagen was the first man to give a detailed description of the mysterious Sete Cidades (Seven Cities) in his book *Antiga Historia do Brasil*, published in 1928. When the second edition of his book came out in 1970, Schwennhagen had long since died a poor schoolmaster.

I first heard the name of Schwennhagen from the lips of Dr Renato Castelo Branco, who brought me an invitation to visit Sete Cidades as the guest of the Government of Piaui.

'Whereabouts are these Sete Cidades?' I asked.

'Only 1,875 miles away as the crow flies,' answered

Dr Branco. 'North of Teresina, between the town of Piripiri and the Rio Longe. We can be there the day after tomorrow.'

There were two reasons why we landed at Teresina at government expense. Firstly, *Chariots of the Gods?* and *Gods from Outer Space* have gone into several editions in South America (especially in Brasil) and open all doors to the author. Secondly, the Governor of Piaui wants to turn the site of Sete Cidades into a national park and is grateful for any publicity which will further his plans.

A well-built road covers the hundred miles from Teresina to Piripiri. The landscape is flat and dark green; the verges of the road are covered with undergrowth that is bordered by dense jungle. Wild pigs, wild cows and wild horses make the journey somewhat dangerous. Although the district is almost on the equator, the climate is bearable. A gentle breeze blows constantly from the coast some 200 miles away. From Piripiri you travel to Sete Cidades by a rough ten-mile road that can be used by cross-country vehicles. Suddenly and without warning you are confronted by the first ruins. (Fig. 43.)

Well, ruins is not quite the right word here. There are no disordered remains of stones that were once built up in layers. There are no monoliths with sharp edges and artificially carved furrows as on the Bolivian plateau at Tiahuanaco. Even after making an intensive search and using your imagination to the full, you can find neither steps, nor stairs, nor streets which could have been lined with houses. Sete Cidades is one monstrous chaos, like the biblical Gomorrah that was destroyed by heaven with fire and brimstone. Stone has been dried out, destroyed, melted by apocalyptic forces. And it must have been a very very long time since the titanic conflagration raged.

No one has ever excavated here.

Science has never attempted to uncover the different strata of this primordial stone past.

Here bizarre stone shapes, articulated monsters, shoot from the ground like question-marks.

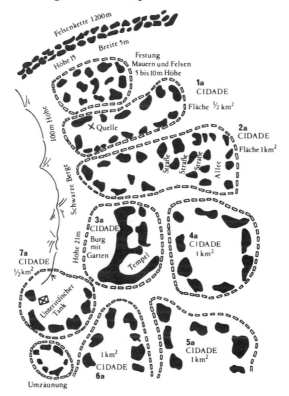

Fig. 43. Plan of Sete Cidades (Seven Cities), which clearly shows order among the chaos of rocks destroyed by apocalyptic forces.

An educated guide, attached to me by the Governor of Piaui, told me that the Seven Cities' strange contorted shapes had been formed by glacial deposits. As I know perfectly well from my home-country Switzerland, when glaciers all over the world withdraw, they leave behind an unmistakable broad band of eroded stone. There are no such traces here. Sete Cidades describes a fairly accurate circle with a diameter of 12 miles. My guide put forward another speculation. In the past there had been a sea-basin here and the Seven Cities were simply the remains of washed out stone; wind and temperature changes had sculpted the strange picturesque 'ruins'. (Fig. 44.)

It might be true. Why not?

I have seen with my own eyes some of the fantastic structures which have come into being through the inventiveness and inexhaustible potentialities of nature. Death Valley in the USA, the Salt Cathedral in Colombia, the granite cauldron in Bolivia and the bizarre, almost architecturally articulated rock fissures on the Dead Sea—they were all wonderful and bizarre enough. There are many

Fig. 44. Detail of the ruined site of Sete Cidades, where the arrangement in seven districts can still be distinguished in spite of the chaos. So far no scientific investigation of the foundations has been undertaken.

strange follies made by the great master-builder, nature.

But in some inexplicable way everything seemed to be quite different at Sete Cidades.

The arrangement of the 'ruins' into seven districts can be clearly seen on the 'official map' of Sete Cidades. Coincidence? A caprice of nature? I cannot accept that so much *deliberate* arrangement was caused by natural forces and I felt it much more likely that a definite plan lay behind it all. But what disconcerted me most were the crumb-like bits of metal squashed between the layers of rock and protruding from them that left traces of rust like long tears on the walls. This feature occurred too often and too regularly in the midst of all the chaos. It is possible that there may be a geological explanation for the 'tortoise' (fig. 45), the special attraction of Sete Cidades, but in the absence of research we know nothing.

Although the origin of the Seven Cities is still unexplained, the rock paintings are an established fact. You can see them and photograph them. And there can be no doubt that the paintings are considerably more recent than the rough weather-worn stone monuments. Sete Cidades has two 'pasts': one a dark primordial past that can probably never be reconstructed and a 'modern' one, although even that dates to prehistoric times.

Once again not even the cleverest man on earth knows *who* painted the paintings on the walls. Yet it very soon becomes clear that the prehistoric artists, with few exceptions, liked to use the same motifs and symbols as are found in cave and rock paintings all over the world. Circles, wheels (with spokes), the sun, concentric circles, squares inside circles and variations on crosses and stars. Just as if all prehistoric artists, even those in the most remote parts, had visited the same art school!

In his book *Kult Symbol Schrift*, Oswald O. Tobisch has

Fig. 45. The 'tortoise' is the special attraction in the wilderness of Sete Cidades. In the absence of research, nothing positive can be said about it.

shown in tabulated form that rock drawings in Africa, Europe, Asia and America are related to each other. At the end of his comparative studies Tobisch asks in amazement:

'Is it possible that once there was a unified concept of God on an international scale simply inconceivable to our present way of thinking and that mankind in those days was still in the "field of force" of the "primordial revelation" of the one and almighty creator, to whom mind and matter, the whole universe with the heavenly bodies and living creatures, were and are subordinate?'

Here I am only going to introduce a few examples of the rock paintings at Sete Cidades, but I shall be glad to place my extensive collection of colour photographs at the disposal of research workers.

The *red and yellow circles*, which are obviously some kind of signal, are noteworthy, especially because rock paintings in two colours are rare. Undoubtedly they were intended to transmit some special message. (Fig. 46.)

The technical sketch shaped something like a test-tube

Fig. 46. The red and yellow circles, obviously a kind of signal, are striking.

in the lower half of which two ropes with signal flags are recognisable, is remarkable (and so far has no counterpart elsewhere). On a sturdy blood-red staff, 12½ ins. high, there are five ovals like the balls on Christmas trees. Nothing from the real world of prehistoric men —animals, plants, stars—can have served as a model for them. (Fig. 47.)

Then there is a line, below which *four balls* dangle like notes of music. As prehistoric men did not know any musical notation—who can deny that?—they must also

Fig. 47. This technical looking plan is remarkable and to the best of my knowledge without parallel in the international catalogue of rock and cave paintings. A test-tube?

be meant to convey a message. There is an ancient Indian relief with nine 'notes of music' below and two above the central line that is almost a counterpart to it. Indian research workers easily identified the relief from descriptions in Sanskrit texts as the representation of a

Fig. 48. The drawing high up on a rock face at Sete Cidades is identical in style and lay-out with an old Indian bas-relief which was identified by Sanskrit scholars as a *Vimaana*, a flying machine.

Vimaana, i.e. a flying machine. (*Gods from Outer Space.*)

Another very remarkable example, in my opinion, was a *flying-machine* (fig. 49) that might have been drawn by a child. Prehistoric painters stylised everything they saw in an extremely simple way. What served them as a 'model' here?

But to me the most extraordinary and impressive painting was a wall with *astronauts* on it. It shows two figures with round helmets, and floating above them a thing that visionaries would call a UFO. A spiral winds between the figures. Next to it a form is reproduced that an imaginative mind could interpret in a limitless number of ways.

A difficult kind of rebus. What can it be? A *space station in orbit*? (fig. 50) A circular band with little windows on the side facing us . . . a band with a protuberance . . . with a bifurcation above it. I have gone over the outlines of the drawing with charcoal to make it clearer. Last but not least, a primitive drawing which shows an *astronaut* in a complete spacesuit. In the company of Ernst von Khuon, I ask the question: were the gods astronauts?

The place where these rock paintings were found is

Fig. 49. Rock and cave painters always stylised objects in their perceptual world. What was the model for this simple *flying machine?*

also very strange and (so far) inexplicable. All the examples of rock drawings reproduced here float at a height of 26 ft. on a very inaccessible wall. I think that the painters (provided there were no giants!) stood on a platform of stone blocks while they were working. But with the passage of time this platform must have been worn away by weathering because there is absolutely no

Fig. 50. A tricky puzzle to solve. A space station in orbit? Concentric circles with little windows? One of the most puzzling finds at Sete Cidades!

trace of it to be found below the high wall. The weathering away of the platform *could* be a clue to the great age of the rock paintings at Sete Cidades.

The reserves of the Hopi Indians, members of the large Pueblo group are located in Arizona and New Mexico. Today there are still about 8,000 Hopis in existence. They weave extremely beautiful baskets, following an ancient handicraft tradition, and make magnificent pottery. In spite of the pressure of the blessings of civilisation, the Hopi Indians on their reserves have preserved their age-old rites and customs, as well as their orally transmitted legends in an astonishingly pure form.

White Bear is chieftain of the Coyote clan by right of birth. He can still read most of the ancient 'drawings'

Fig. 51. Large numbers of petroglyphs can be seen on the rocks of the reserve, although they are often hard to get at. Of the four sketches chosen, the 'Star Blower' is the most striking. Antenna-like attributes can easily be recognised.

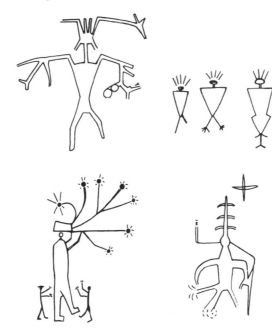

carved in the rock. Thus White Bear knows that a hand with outspread fingers next to the paintings means that the tribe who once executed the drawings is still in possession of the whole traditional wisdom. White Bear is capable of interpreting widely separated rock and cave drawings that he has never seen before. Unfortunately the chieftain is very reticent and extremely sceptical of white men (with good reason). The petroglyphs in the reserves are of remarkable design and sometimes whole rock faces are covered with them. (Fig. 51.)

What have the legends of the Hopi Indians to tell us?

They say that the first world was Toktela. (Toktela literally means *infinite space*.) Only Taiowa, the creator, originally dwelt in the first world before he created men. The ancestors had been in contact with various worlds before they found their home on this planet. Taiowa told them that the supreme law was 'Thou shalt not kill'. If there were any differences of opinion or disputes between the Hopis, the opposing parties separated, went off in different directions and sought new hunting grounds. But both sides stuck to the traditional laws and kept on covering rocks and caves with the same paintings during their long marches. (They still observe this practice today.)

In the *Book of the Hopi* (the first revelation of the Hopi's historical and religious world-view of life) the following legend is told:

'In ancient times there was a battle for the Red City in the South. Wherever they came from, all the tribes were accompanied by Kachinas, beings who were reputed not to be of the 'fourth world', indeed, they were not men at all. Nevertheless, they always proved themselves to be protectors and advisors of the tribe and frequently helped them out of tricky situations with superhuman powers and arts. This was what happened in the Red City in the South when some Hopi tribes were suddenly attacked from all sides. With the speed of the wind, the Kachinas built a tunnel through which the Hopis were able to flee into the open behind the enemy lines without shedding blood. When they said goodbye, the Kachinas said to the chieftains: "We are staying to defend the city. The time for the journey to *our distant planet* has not yet come!" '

If we follow the Hopi traditions, all the red rock drawings are simply very early messages with precise instructions to tribe members who might happen to pass through that particular bit of territory at any given time.

It would be an interesting experiment to show Big Chief White Bear my colour photographs of rock and cave drawings at Sete Cidades. Who knows, perhaps he would 'read' in the remarkably similar symbols and motifs that the mysterious Red City of the South had been rediscovered at last.

Fig. 52. I met Felicitas Barreto, the celebrated Indian scholar, at Teresina. She has lived in the jungle with Indians on the banks of the Rio Paru for 20 years.

Back in Teresina, I looked forward keenly to a meeting with Felicitas Barreto (fig. 52), a Brasilian who is an Indian scholar of high standing. Her book *Danzas Indigenas del Brasil* (Native Dances of Brasil), with descriptions of the ritual dances of various wild Indian tribes, had made a deep impression on me. We had been in correspondence for some years and now I was going to meet her in person. Mrs Barreto, 'lost' to civilisation for 20 years, came from the godforsaken region of the Upper Rio Paru, on the borders of Brasil and French Guyana. The Brasilian Air Force was bringing her to Belem. I had guaranteed a return flight from there to Teresina.

'Good heavens, how noisy it is in this town! Can't we creep into some quiet corner?' said Mrs Barreto, a middle-aged lady with a wiry figure. I found the quietest room in the Hotel Nacional. Below I reproduce some of the conversation I took down on my tape-recorder:

'How long is it since you have been in a town?'

'About twenty months, but one day will last me for a very long time. Already I'm homesick away from my Indians in the virgin forest.'

'Homesick?'

'Yes, for nature. I've learnt to converse silently with the sticks and stones, with animals and dewdrops. The Indians don't talk much, but we understand each other perfectly.'

'You live among wild Indians. Why don't they kill you, since you're a white woman?'

'The Indians don't live up to their reputation, and anyway I am a woman, and a woman is like a snake without venom, like a weapon without a point. They call me "pale half-moon" because of my blonde hair. All the tribes know about me, they all know me by that name and if I move on to another tribe, I am always given a friendly reception.'

'What do you wear? Jeans?'

'Good lord, no! Mostly I go about naked or in a grass skirt. The chief of the tribe I'm studying now has invited me to be his third wife.'

'For heaven's sake! Surely you haven't said yes?'

'Not yet, but it would be nice to be a chief's third wife. As third wife I should have the least work to do. Besides, three of us could give the chief a sound thrashing.'

'Really?'

'Yes, why not? If an Indian does not treat his wives properly or plays tricks on them, his wives beat him. After he has had his beating, he has to leave the house, go to the river and stay there in a kneeling position. If none of his wives fetch him before evening, he has to spend that night and all the following nights in the men's house and look for new wives. Perhaps these strict customs are the reason why Indians are perfect gentlemen. And I must add that the tribe never deserts anyone, even if he is being ostracised or is seriously ill. Twice I was bitten by poisonous snakes; I lost consciousness for several days and the Indians looked after me and cured me with plants which they chewed and applied to the wound.'

'You know my books. What do the Indians have to say about the idea that man comes from the universe?'

'Let me answer your question with a legend that is told by the Kaiato tribe. They live on the Upper Xingu in the State of Mato Grosso. Incidentally all the tribes know this legend or similar ones.'

'Far away from here on an alien star sat an Indian council that decided to change the tribe's dwelling place. The Indians began to dig a hole in the ground, deeper and deeper, until it came out on the other side of their planet. The chief was the first to rush into the hole and after a long cold night he came to the earth, but the air resistance there was so strong that it blew the chief back again to his old home. Then the chief told the tribal council about his experience, that he had seen a beautiful blue world with a lot of water and many green woods and that he advised that all Indians should go to this world. The council decided to follow the chief's advice and ordered the Indians to plait a long cotton cord. On this cord they slowly lowered themselves into the hole so that they too would not be blown back from the earth. Because they entered the earth's atmosphere slowly, their mass migration was successful and since then they have lived on earth. In the beginning, relate the Kaiato, contact was still maintained with the old home through the cord, but one day a wicked magician cut it in two and since then they have been waiting for their brothers and sisters from their old home to seek and find them again on the earth.'

'Do the Indians also speak about the stars?'

'Not about the stars, but to the stars! They often sit motionless in a circle for hours, holding each other by the shoulder as in an endless chain and not saying a word. If you ask one of the men who was present (after the session is over) what they all did, you would certainly not get an answer, but I know from the women that the men are conversing with heaven.'

'Are they praying then?'

'No, they are carrying on silent dialogues with someone up there.' Mrs Barreto hunched her shoulders and pointed to the ceiling.

'Tell me, do the wild Indians still have any rites or ritual objects that point to any kind of connection with the universe?'

'O yes! There are the feathered men, Indians who cover themselves with feathers from head to foot, to make themselves look like birds who can rise into the cosmos so easily. And then there are the countless types of masks, which, if one likes, can all be interpreted along the lines of your theories. Many of the masks have branches with several forks springing from them like the antennae in your cave drawings. Often the Indians completely disguise themselves in straw to make themselves resemble their fabulous ancestors. Joao Americo Peret, one of our outstanding Indian scholars, recently published some photographs of Kayapo Indians in ritual clothing that he took as long ago as 1952, long before Gagarin's first spaceflight! If you look at those photographs, the first thing you think of is astronauts. The Kayapos, not to be confused with the Kaiato, live in the south of the State of Para on the Rio Fresco.'

João Americo Peret very kindly allowed me to use copies of his photographs of Kayapos in their 'ritual garments' as illustrations to this book. (Fig. 53.) He took them in an Indian village on the Rio Fresco, south of

Fig. 53. Dr João Americo Peret took these photos of Kayapo Indians in 1952, when no one had any idea how astronauts dressed. The Indians wear these ritual robes in memory of the appearance of the heavenly being Bep Kororoti.

Para. In view of this really astonishing masquerade I feel that it is important to re-emphasise that Peret took these photographs in 1952 at a time when the clothing and equipment of astronauts were still not familiar to all us Europeans, let alone these wild Indians! Yuri Gagarin orbited the earth in his spaceship Vostok I for the first time on 12 April, 1961, and only since that event have astronauts in their suits become as familiar a sight as mannequins in shop windows. The Kayapos in their straw imitation spacesuits need no commentary apart from the remark that these 'ritual garments' have been worn by the Indian men of this tribe on festive occasions since time immemorial, according to Peret.

The Kayapo legend that João Americo Peret told me needs no commentary either. Peret heard it in the village of Gorotire on the banks of the Fresco from the Indian Kuben Kran Kein, the old counsellor of the tribe, who bears the title of Gway Baba, the wise. This is the legend which the sage related:

'Our people lived in a big savanna, far away from this region, from which one could see the mountain range Pukato Ti, the summits of which were enveloped in a cloud of uncertainty and this uncertainty has not been cleared to this day. The sun, tired from its long daily walk, lay down on the green grass behind the brushwood and Mem Baba, the inventor of all things, covered the heaven with his cloak full of hanging stars. When a star falls down, Memi Keniti traverses heaven and takes it back to the right place. That is the task of Memi Keniti, the eternal guardian.

One day, Bep Kororoti, who came from the Pukato Ti mountains, arrived in the village for the first time. He was clad in a *bo* (i.e. the straw suit in the pictures), which covered him from head to foot. He carried a *kop*, a thunder weapon, in his hand. Everyone in the village was terrified and fled into the bush. The men tried to protect the women and children, and some of them attempted to fight the intruder, but their weapons were too weak for they crumbled to dust every time they touched Bep Kororoti. The warrior who had come from the cosmos must have laughed at the weakness of those who fought against him. To demonstrate his strength he raised his *kop*, pointed it first at a tree and then at a stone, and destroyed them both. Everyone believed that in so doing Bep Kororoti wanted to show them that he had not come to wage war with them.

Confusion reigned for a long time. The bravest warriors of the tribe tried to organise resistance, but in the end they could only succumb to the presence of Bep Kororoti, for he did no harm to them. His beauty, the radiant whiteness of his skin, his obvious affection and love gradually enchanted everyone. They felt safe with him and became friends.

Bep Kororoti took pleasure in learning how to use our weapons and how to become a good hunter. He progressed so well that he could handle our weapons better than the best men of the tribe and was braver than the bravest men in the village. It did not take long before Bep Kororoti was received into the tribe as a warrior and then a young maiden sought him as a husband and married him. They begot sons and a daughter, whom they called Nio Pouti.

Bep Kororoti was more clever than anyone else so he began to instruct the others in unknown matters. He led the men in the construction of a Ng Obi, the men's house that all our villages have today. In it the men told the youngsters about their adventures and so they learnt how to behave when in danger and how to think. In truth the house was a school and Bep Kororoti was the teacher.

In the Ng Obi handicrafts were developed and our
weapons were improved and there was nothing that
we do not owe to the great warrior from the universe.
It was he who founded the "big chamber" in which we
discussed the trials and needs of our tribe, and thus a
better organisation came into being that made life and
work easier for everybody.

Often the younger men resisted and did not go to
the Ng Obi. Then Bep Kororoti put on his *bo* and
sought the young men; once he had done this they
could no longer resist and came quickly back to the Ng
Obi because only there were they safe.

If hunting was difficult, Bep Kororoti fetched his *kop*
and killed the animals without damaging them. The
hunter was always allowed to take the best piece of
prey for himself, but Bep Kororoti, who did not eat the
village food, only took what was essential to feed his
family. His friends did not approve of this, but he did
not change his attitude.

His behaviour did change with the years. He no
longer went out with the others. He wanted to stay in
his hut. But when he did leave his hut he always went
up into the mountains of Pukato Ti from which he had
come. One day he followed the will of his spirit, for he
could no longer master it. He left the village. He
assembled his family and only Nio Pouti was not present, for she was away, and his departure followed
rapidly. The days passed and Bep Kororoti was not to
be found. But suddenly he reappeared in the village
square and uttered a terrifying war cry. Everyone
thought he had gone mad and they all tried to calm
him down. But when the men tried to approach him, a
terrible battle took place. Bep Kororoti did not use his
weapons, but his body trembled and anyone who
touched him fell to the ground dead. The warriors
died in swarms.

The battle lasted for days, then the fallen groups of warriors could stand up again and continued to try to subdue Bep Kororoti. They pursued him almost to the crest of the mountains. Then something happened that left everyone speechless. Bep Kororoti walked backwards to the far edge of the Pukato Ti. With his *kop* he destroyed everything that was near him. By the time he had reached the very top of the mountain range, trees and bushes had turned to dust. Suddenly there was a tremendous crash that shook the whole region and Bep Kororoti vanished into the air, surrounded by fiery clouds, smoke and thunder. By this earth-shaking event the roots of the bushes were torn from the ground and the wild fruits destroyed. Game disappeared so that the tribe began to suffer from hunger.

Nio Pouti, who had married a warrior and bore a son, and was as we know a daughter of the heavenly Bep Kororoti, told her husband that she knew where food for the whole tribe could be found, but first they would have to follow her into the mountains to Pukato Ti. Urged on by Nio Pouti her husband plucked up courage and followed her into the region of Pukato Ti. There she looked for a special tree in the district of Mem Baba Kent Kre and sat on its branches with her son in her lap. Then she told her husband to bend the branches of the tree down till their tips touched the ground. At the moment that this contact took place, there was a big explosion and Nio Pouti disappeared amid clouds, smoke, dust, thunder and lightning.

Her husband waited for a few days. He had lost his courage and was almost dying of hunger when he heard a crash and saw the tree standing in its old place again. His surprise was great, his wife was there again and with her Bep Kororoti and they brought with them big baskets full of food such as he did not know and had never seen. After a time the heavenly man sat in the fantastic tree again and ordered him to bend the boughs down to the earth. There was an explosion and the tree disappeared into the air again.

Nio Pouti returned to the village with her husband and made known an order of Bep Kororoti's. Everyone must leave immediately and erect their villages in front of Baba Kent Kre where they would get their food. Nio Pouti also said that they had to keep the seeds of fruit and vegetables and bushes until the rainy season so that they could put them in the earth again and reap new harvests.

That is how agriculture started . . . Our people moved to Pukato Ti and lived there in peace; the huts of our villages grew more numerous and they could be seen stretching from the mountains right up to the horizon . . .'

I had this Kayapo legend, which was told me by the Indian scholar João Americo Peret, translated literally from the Portuguese. Equally old as the legend is the straw spacesuit which the Indians wear in memory of the appearance of Bep Kororoti.

6: *Rarities, Curiosities and Speculations*

In 1863 the American diplomat E. G. Squire found a human skull that was dated to about 2000 B.C. at Cuzco in the Andean plateau in Peru. A rectangular piece of bone had been chiselled out of the skull. Squire gave his find to the French anthropologist Paul Broca (1824–1880), who was the first man to localise the seat of speech in a convolution in the front part of the brain (the convolution of Broca). Broca found six extremely fine wires in the hollow skull and diagnosed a bone infection, which led him to conclude that an operation had been performed on the skull during the patient's lifetime.

According to this, skull operations are by no means epoch-making surgical interventions of our own time. The strange thing is that even modern men shudder when they read reports about brain operations. Everyone should be pleased when medicine makes progress which can liberate mankind from old afflictions. I should like to show that the essential needs arising out of plans for future space travel are an important stimulus to medical research.

Professor Robert Y. White, the neuro-surgeon, works in the Metropolitan General Hospital, Cleveland, USA. The goal of this grand old man of brain surgery is to tackle that scourge of mankind, the stroke, by operating on the brain. White builds on the research of his colleagues at Keo University, Tokyo, who perform operations with the brain chilled to a temperature of about 6°C. With a body temperature of 36°C. a surgeon has three minutes at most in which to operate. For some years White experimented with supercooled monkeys'

151

brains. The news that during these experiments White had succeeded in keeping the brain of a rhesus monkey alive for three days when separated from its body hit the headlines in specialist medical journals. White kept the solo brain supplied by attaching its blood-vessels to the carotid artery of a living member of the same species. Herbert L. Schrader, who was present at one experiment, wrote:

'The isolated monkey's brain is alive. It emits electric currents ordering action like every living brain. It can have sensations, pain, fear . . . Perhaps it sleeps as well, perhaps it dreams. What is still left of the monkey's personality cannot see, cannot hear, cannot smell, cannot feel. The brain can receive no information from the outside world, because all the sensory nerves have been cut off short. Nor can it run away because it no longer has a body to carry out its orders. But it can issue orders, for the nerve centre is intact and receives a good supply of blood—from the blood of another monkey. No one knows what goes on in such a brain, for no one has managed to decipher the traces left by its electric impulses. Consequently, even for the research worker it is only an organised bundle of many millions of nerve cells which have a metabolism and send out currents.'

Professor White's collaborators are of the opinion that the functions of a brain separated from the body react more accurately and quicker than those of a brain 'burdened' with the whole organism. In its solo state it is still only a centre of stored information that it has received from the limbs and organs, but it is absolutely intact and capable of initiating new actions at lightning speed.

The inevitable development of such series of experiments is to couple a solo brain to a computer. Thus the Californian brain specialist Dr Lawrence Pinneo replaced a small part of a monkey's brain by a computer. It was then possible to control the animal's arm movements through the intermediary of the computer.

Professor José Delgado of Yale University went a stage further. He sank several probes into the aggression centre of the brain of Paddy, a female monkey, and in addition put a tiny radio transmitter under the skin of her head. If Paddy got furious, Delgado pressed some buttons on the control set and the lady monkey (who incidentally suffered no pain throughout the whole process) at once became as quiet as a lamb.

The London brain surgeon Professor Giles Brindley is already working on human brains. Brindley implanted eighty tiny electrodes in the soft brain matter of a blind old lady and she can already recognise geometrical figures again. At the University Clinic in New Orleans, three men had electrodes implanted in their sexual centre. Using a control set which they could carry in their trousers pockets or hide under their pillows, they could be in fighting form for the sexual act in a flash. These technical aphrodisiacs may have a tremendous future in our stress-troubled male world.

Bio-engineering is still a very young offshoot of the established sciences, but it is coming on rapidly under the pressure of necessity. The development of bio-engineering is still in its infancy. Will it succeed in building a Cyborg, a combination of solo brain and computer? Undoubtedly it will. Dr R. M. Page, Director of the US Naval Research Laboratory, has seriously discussed the project of feeding a computer with ideas, plans and commands via a solo brain—free of all influences. When is this project to become reality? Professor Robert L. Sinsheimer, California Institution of Technology, Pasadena, USA, has this general observation to make:

'The history of the natural sciences and technology

has shown, especially in this century, that scientists, particularly the conservative ones, have nearly always erred when they tried to predict the rate at which the new theoretical findings of scientific research are put into practise.'

The Cyborg will inevitably have to come, because the dozen milliard nerve cells, multiplied by the hundred milliard cells in the supporting web of the nervous system, are the only ones in a position to store and make use of the knowledge of the present for the future. What the $45\frac{1}{2}$ to 64 oz. of our brain mass really contains will not be known until there has been much more work in this broad new field of research. It will take a Cyborg to show that until now only a small fraction of the tremendous storage capacity of our grey cells has been used.

It should need no commentary to make clear how important brain research and brain surgery are for the well-being of mankind. But it is also obvious how important these results of medical research are for future space travel. There are two possibilities for the technical reach for the stars. If we do not succeed during the next decades in building propulsion units which can take spaceships close to the speed of light (186,283 miles per second), then a journey by human astronauts even to the nearest fixed star, Proxima Centauri, is impossible. It is 4.3 light years away from us and 3,000 terrestrial years of cosmic flight are an absurd conception. However, time as the giant hurdle in the way of successful cosmic flight *can* be overcome by the Cyborg. The solo brain, linked to a computer and given a constant supply of blood, will be the control centre of a spaceship. In the view of Roger A. McGowan, a practical scientist, the Cyborg will be developed into an electronic being whose functions are programmed in a solo brain and transformed into orders by the brain. The Cyborg does not change, does not fall ill, does not catch cold, has no lapses of memory. It would be the ideal commanding officer of a spaceship. And the unbridgeable gap between us and the stars out of a sea of time would be spanned.

The leaps in the technical development of space travel are so enormous that it is useful to remember that the first measurements near the moon were made by the unmanned satellite Lunik 2 on 13 September, 1959. Manned spaceships did not begin their journeys to the moon until ten years later, from 1969 onwards.

Up to that date, the year that opened up the heavens, the following were the successfully launched *unmanned* spaceflights.

	USA	USSR
In orbit round the earth	529	272
Moon hits	12	6
Moon orbits	6	5
Venus hits	—	2
Sun orbits	11	8
. . . and these *manned* spaceflights		
Flights	15	9
Times round earth	840	310
Flying hours in space	2773	533

In the spring of 1973 Skylab, the first world space station and Wernher von Braun's 'favourite child', will leave Houston.

Whereas on all the previous Apollo flights every pound of weight was grudged—each pound of payload needed 2,360 lb. of fuel—Skylab will offer a degree of comfort on its four-week journey through space that might have been invented by science-fiction authors. It will be 45 ft. long and 19½ ft. wide, and the astronauts will have a workroom and a sleeping cabin at their disposal, not to mention a bathroom supplied from a tank containing 600 gallons of water. The refrigerators hold a ton of selected foodstuffs. The astronauts will not only be in permanent contact with Houston by radio and television as before, they will also be able to type the results of their scientific missions on 160 rolls of telex paper and telex them to earth. And so that the astronauts do not have to wear the same clothes all the time, Skylab will have an extensive wardrobe with 60 items of clothing.

What an outcry I should have heard if I had foretold Skylab for 1973 in *Chariots of the Gods* in 1968!

Pioneer F, the American spaceship which is to report on Jupiter, was the first man made flying object planned to leave our solar system. In March 1972 it shot from the launching pad at Cape Kennedy on a journey that may last 100,000,000 years. After approximately 360 days, at the end of February 1973, Pioneer F will pass the biggest planet in our solar system, Jupiter (diameter 88,700 miles). With a mass 318 times as big as the earth's Jupiter is bigger than all the other planets put together.

Then Pioneer F will leave our solar system.

The launching of the ship alone with a weight of nearly 600 lb. caused a sensation in the technology of space travel. With a three-stage Atlas Centaur rocket it had to be accelerated to 32,500 miles per hour so that the right ballistic curve—passing Jupiter with extreme accuracy —could be reached. This feat has broken all speed records. Pioneer F has an especially significant technical novelty on board. As sunlight in the vicinity of Jupiter has only 1/27th of the force it has on earth, it has not been possible to build solar batteries for storing the sun's energy. For the first time a tiny atomic power-station will be constructed for Pioneer F. The reactors will be driven by plutonium 238 dioxide and the energy produced will suffice with its wattage to send radio signals to earth on the 28 billiard $(= 10^{15})$ kilometre-long space flight.

The data that Pioneer F will supply, however important they may be at the beginning of the age of enquiry and research into the outer planets, do not interest me as much as the aluminium and gold plaquette that Pioneer F has on board. The American astrophysicist and exobiologist Carl Sagan of Cornell University and Frank Drake of the United States Astronomical Research Centre persuaded NASA that a gold-covered aluminium plaque measuring 6 ins. by 12 ins. by $\frac{1}{2}$ in. should be placed in the ship so that extra-terrestrial intelligences that might encounter Pioneer F could extract information from it. (Fig. 54.)

The text of the message could not be written in any of the languages known to us, because it is a 100% certain that it would not be understood. So Sagan and Drake developed a sign language which in their view

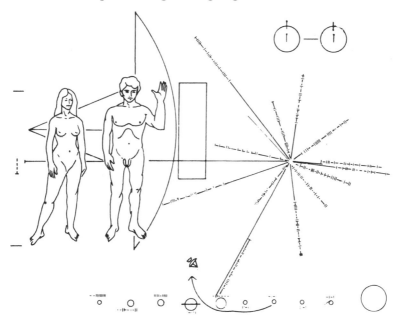

Fig. 54. This is the gold and aluminium plaque which Pioneer F took with it as a message to alien intelligences on its journey of 9,461 billion kilometres. Carl Sagan and Frank Drake worked out a 'cosmic' script.

ought to be intelligible to all thinking beings.

What should the plaque's message be?

It should say where Pioneer F came from; who sent Pioneer F out into space; when it was launched and what its home planet was, among other things.

At the foot of the plaque there is a picture of the sun and its nine planets, an 'image' that does not have to be deciphered, as every intelligence knows them. The distances of the planets from the sun are given in binary numbers. For example, if Mercury has a distance from the sun of ten binary units (expressed by 10 10), the earth is 26 units, or 11 0 10, distant from the sun. As the binary system of counting is the 'language' of all logically constructed computers, Sagan and Drake say that it is the one that could be most readily understood by alien intelligences. On the right of the plaque the outline of Pioneer F on its flight path from earth to Jupiter is schematically engraved. Above it are a man and a woman in a standing position. The man raises his right hand in the peace sign. The left half shows the position of the sun with 14 lines, cosmic sources of energy, which are supposed to explain by the sun's position both the launching date and the home of the ship using binary notations. An atom of hydrogen, which has been proved to have an identical structure in all worlds is drawn in the upper left-hand corner as the 'key' to deciphering all the information. An alien intelligence (provided it thought in a technical way) could even work out the size of the woman's body from it! The wavelength of the hydrogen atom in spectrum analysis (which radiates symbolically from the sun on the plaque with a line 23.3 cm. long) is multiplied by the binary figure 10 00, which is marked next to the lady and corresponds to an '8'. This gives $8 \times 20.3 = 162.4$, and that is the height of the Eve on the plaque: 162.4 cm.!

I met Dr Frank Drake in New York and asked him

why the aluminium plaque had been covered with a layer of gold.

'In theory the ship can cover 28 billiard kilometres. It may be 3,000 light years en route (a light year is the distance covered by light in a year and light travels at 186,000 miles a second). If we want to ensure that our plaque can still be deciphered by someone after its long journey, we have to protect it from corrosion with a precious metal. Aluminium covered with gold was the cheapest.'

'For whom is the information on the plaque intended?'

'For any intelligence who happens to locate the ship and then undertakes to examine and interpret it. Sagan and I consider the very fact that we could equip Pioneer F with a cosmic message is a hopeful sign that our civilisation is interested enough in the future to actually send out information and not merely await a sign from the universe.'

I think that Sagan and Drake's enterprise provides a chance of passing information to intelligent scientists on distant planets.

But what happens if this Pioneer plaque lands in a civilisation that understands nothing of binary arithmetic and computer technology? Will our unknown brothers in space look on the gold and aluminium plaque as an extraordinary present from the gods up in heaven? Will our alien brothers teach their children to make similar 'images'? Will they themselves make imitations and set them up in their temples? Will archaeologists claim, even out there in space, that the copies are ritual objects? Who knows what other interpretations might be given to the Cape Kennedy plaque?

If scientists in the year 1972 send two naked members of our species, plus suns, lines and circles, into the universe on a shining plaque, why should not extra-terrestrial beings 3,000 light years away have brought *us* similar messages or variations of them on a similar journey. If I put the Pioneer F's plaque next to the Inca gold plaque and compare the signs under a magnifying glass, I ask myself why someone does not begin to examine and check all these circles, lines, zigzags, squares and dotted lines with the eyes of space-age men. Perhaps they could even be deciphered. (Fig. 55.)

Surely the chances of success would make it worth the effort?

In *Chariots of the Gods?* I briefly mentioned the possibility that the speed of light might not necessarily be the upper limit of all velocity. This frivolous suggestion was met with icy silence, because everyone knew that Einstein had proved that there was nothing faster than light. Einstein has shown that light is a universal constant. Nevertheless, he takes the factor t = time into account in his formula. For example, the time in a rocket passes more quickly or slowly depending on the condition of motion; distances alter and the upper limit of the speed of light shifts. This says *nothing* counter to the theory of relativity, which proves conclusively and for all time that a body which moves below the speed of light can *never* exceed the speed of light with an expenditure of finite energy. But what happens with the expenditure of infinite energy?

Today physicists and astronomers actually confirm that the speed of light is *not* the upper limit of all motion. Professor Y. A. Wheeler of Princeton University, USA, who is an expert on the relativity theory and was a co-discoverer of the hydrogen bomb, and therefore is no visionary, invented a model of a 'super-space' in which time and the speed of light lose their values. However contradictory it may seem, spaceships in the super-space could be in any desired place without time passing.

Does that mean theoretically all the possibilities for interstellar spaceflight exist? Perhaps. At some time in

Fig. 55. Could this gold plaque be a message from alien astronauts to us? Note the animals (left) and the 'binary' markings. Who will decipher this code? What has it got to tell us?

the future. With the discovery of the subatomic particles called tachyons, luxons and tardyons, a new subatomic world swam into the physicists' ken. All these particles move faster than light within their inertial system (this means a system in which there are no forces to overcome inertia, but in which a body remains in a state of rest or in uniform motion). Tachyons, luxons and tardyons always move faster than light. Consequently existing calculations of energy no longer apply to these particles because they are faster than light 'by nature'. Our world, in which the speed of light is the upper limit of velocity, is *one* inertial system, but the world of tachyons, luxons and tardyons with a velocity faster than light is *another* inertial system.

Physicists know this today, but astronomers have also discovered that the speed of light is not the absolute limit of velocity. A British research group from Oxford University led by Y. S. Allen and Geoffrey Endean came to the conclusion, after many years of study, that the electro-magnetic fields in the Crab nebula in the constellation Taurus must move at a speed of 375,000 miles per second. The celebrated English scientific periodical *Nature* also mentioned the possibility of speeds faster than light.

Yet these new discoveries are merely the first indications of conceivably *infinite* velocities.

How long is it since an *atom* was simply identified as the smallest particle with the qualities of a chemical element, and how old is the knowledge that every piece of matter is composed of an inconceivably large number of atoms? It was in 1913 that the Danish Nobel Prize winner Niels Bohr (1885-1962) laid the foundations of atomic theory with his atomic model. Today atomic energy, obtained from the combined energy of protons and neutrons in the atomic nucleus, is made use of industrially. Atomic energy alone can ensure the world's supply of energy. Mankind became terrifyingly aware of this effective application of a radical physical idea when the USA exploded the first hydrogen bomb near the Marshall Islands in November, 1952—a bomb which was also a product of atomic energy, but whose 'atomic mushroom' image still lowers menacingly over the peaceful use of such energy.

This recent example could be a very practical pointer to how rapidly original discoveries can lead to effective results via the imaginative applications of technicians. At least the stars have become a little bit closer to us with the establishment of faster than light particles.

It is not so long since authors of adventure stories equipped mysterious foreign powers with ray guns which could cut holes in walls, destroy other weapons and vaporise men.

Today these rays exist. Every schoolboy knows them as lasers. The whole secret is an apparatus for light amplification by stimulated emission of radiation using a crystal. Very rapid technological development replaced the ruby originally used by other solid bodies, and even by gas mixtures that continually send out light. The heat at the focussing point of a lens placed in a laser beam is so high that even metals with a high smelting point vaporise. When these rays are directed on to a microscopically fine point, they can be used not only for amplifying light in astronomical telescopes and for the transmission of radio programmes without disturbance, but also for cutting tiny holes in skin-thin metal plates in watch factories. In eye operations they are used to weld detached retinas back on. It is no longer a secret that in both east and west experiments with laser rifles and laser cannon are being carried out.

Could it be that the idea of laser beams is not really so new?

In Exodus xvii, 10–14, I think the text refers fairly clearly to the use of a laser weapon:

> '. . . and Moses, Aaron, and Hur went up to the top of the hill.
>
> And it came to pass, when Moses held up his hand, that Israel prevailed: and when he let down his hand, Amalek prevailed.
>
> But Moses' hands were heavy: and they took a stone, and put it under him, and he stayed thereon; and Aaron and Hur stayed up his hands, the one on the one side, and the other on the other side; and his hands were steady until the going down of the sun.'

What happened here?

In the battle against the Amalekites, the Israelites only went on winning as long as Moses, up on the mountain, kept his arms raised. Now the raised arms of the weary commander *alone* could have been of little use, nor would they have been any more dangerous when the faithful supported them. So I assume that Moses held a rather heavy object in his hands that could decide the battle in his favour. On his field-marshal's hill he had the hostile armies within his field of vision. If he 'hit' the Amalekites with his ray guns, his people conquered, if he let his arms sink (and with them the ray guns), the Amalekites, fighting with old-fashioned weapons, attacked successfully. This speculation of mine gets strong support in the same chapter, verse 9, where it says that Moses stood on the top of the hill '*with the rod of God*' in his hand. Looked at from this point of view, isn't it logical that the battle turned against the Israelites when Moses grew tired and let the ray guns sink?

In *Gods from Outer Space* I included a petroglyph (fig. 56a) from Easter Island which showed a strange figure, half fish, half man. Since then a technically minded reader

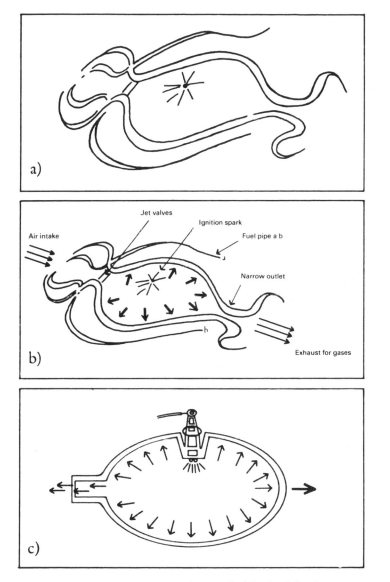

Fig. 56. (a) A petroglyph on the coast of Easter Island.
(b) Interpretation of the drawing as ram-jet propulsion unit.
(c) Section of a modern combustion rocket.

(Horst Haas) has pointed out to me that this drawing on the rock near the shore of Easter Island could easily be the representation of a ram jet engine (fig. 56b). The 'head' of the drawing would be the air intake, the narrow neck the fuel inlet, the paunchlike broadening out the combustion and pressure chamber and the concluding narrow part the exhaust for the high velocity gases, while the engraved star would be a symbol of the ignition spark. In this way the whole drawing would be a stylised model of a ram jet propulsion unit. 'Even if the drawing as a whole does not conform to an aerodynamic shape,' writes Horst Haas, 'perhaps further references to its flying behaviour, etc., could be deduced by accurate measurements of the landing grounds marked out on the plain of Nazca.'

I suggest that the archaeologists ask their colleagues at a technical college for advice for a change!

Easter Island is an island full of puzzles where research would be well worthwhile. In his book *Phantastique Ile de Paques,* Francis Mazière tells of an excavation which brought to light an unknown type of stone head. Whereas the heads of all the other statues are clean shaven, this head sported a beard and it had faceted eyes of the kind insects have (and as we know them from Japanese Dogu sculptures). But the most extraordinary thing was two staves that sprouted from the head. Now if anyone wants to claim that they were symbolical representations of animal horns, they are off target. There have never been horned animals on Easter Island! Even a humorous prehistoric sculptor had no model from which he could copy horns to put on a man! It is ridiculous to deny that prehistoric artists—without drawing on their imagination—carved antennae as they had seen them on the gods who came to them from the cosmos.

Louis Pauwels and Jacques Bergier describe representations of non-human beings wearing technical accoutrements found in a quite different corner of the world. Granite reliefs depicting beings in diving- or spacesuits with 'elephants' trunks' were discovered in the Hunan Mountains (People's Republic of China). We cannot avoid asking ourselves whether these trunks were not really breathing apparatuses. Interpreters of such finds will dismiss the question as absurd, because these trunked men are ascribed a date of 45,000 B.C. Yet every find of this type should worry us because every find increases the certainty of prehistoric visits by alien astronauts. Must the cobbler stick to his old last?

At Delhi there is an ancient iron column that contains no phosphorus or sulphur and so cannot be destroyed by the effects of weathering. However, it is not always necessary to leave the ransacked west to come upon equally wonderful discoveries. At Kottenforst, a few miles west of Bonn, there is an iron column which has been known locally since time immemorial as the Iron Man, writes Dr Harro Grubert of Cologne. The iron column rises 4 ft. 10 ins. out of the ground, but according to various estimates and magnetic resistance measurements it sticks 90 ft. deep into the ground. The part above ground exhibits slight surface weathering, but surprisingly enough no trace of rust. The column (fig. 57) is first mentioned in a fourteenth-century document, where it is described as marking a village boundary. In the immediate vicinity of the iron column lie a well-built stone walk and the remains of an aqueduct, which does not—wonder of wonders—run in the usual direction Eifel-Bonn or Eifel-Cologne, but straight towards the column. So far no one knows what to make of the long rectangular column, and people know a lot about iron in this part of the world. Why should not metallurgists spare the time to travel to that developing country India to check whether or not the iron column in the temple courtyard at Delhi has a similar alloy to the strange column at Kottenforst? Such factual *knowledge* might produce evidence as to the age of both columns, for I think it is absurd to accept the Iron Man as being no more than a village boundary mark. If

Fig. 57. The Iron Man at Kottenforst near Bonn is embedded 90 ft. in the ground. There is a similar iron column at Delhi. In spite of their age, neither of them has rusted!

it were, why should it stick 90 ft. into the ground? Central Europe, too, may have been *one* goal of 'visits by the gods' and then the Iron Man's real significance would emerge.

There *used to be* a rarity in Salzburg, too. Johannes V. Butlar says:

'Who knows how to solve the mystery of Dr Gurlt's dice. It was the strangest object ever discovered in a block of coal from the Tertiary, where it was enclosed for many millions of years. This almost perfect dice was found in 1885. There was a deep incision round its middle and two parallel outer surfaces were rounded off. It consisted of a hard alloy of coal and nickel steel and weighed 785 grammes. Its sulphur content was too low for it to have come from natural gravel, which occasionally occurs in remarkable geometrical shapes. Scientists were never able to agree about the dice's origin. It was preserved in the Salzburg Museum until 1910 and then disappeared mysteriously. Mystery piled on mystery!'

If the dice came from the Tertiary, I can only ask did monkeys know a process for making steel?

The print of a shoe was found in a coal seam in Fisher Canyon, Nevada. The impression of the sole is so clear, says Andrew Thomas, that even traces of strong thread are recognisable. The age of this shoeprint is estimated as 15,000,000 years. 'Man did not appear until another 13,000,000 years had passed. To put it in other words, primitive man, in the generally accepted view appeared about 2,000,000 years ago and first began to wear shoes 20,000 years ago. So whose footprint can it be?

I can only answer the question with suppositions. Either the monkeys made shoes and plaited soles (in

which case the horizontal profession is not the oldest profession in the world!), or beings who already knew that
shoes were the ideal protection for the feet walked the
earth millions of years ago.

In 1972 the English archaeologist Professor Walter
Bryan Emery found a lump of limestone in an underground passage near Sakkara in Egypt. As the scholar
carefully scraped it, a statuette of the sun god Osiris
appeared. Suddenly Professor Emery felt a stabbing pain
and collapsed. Myocardial infarction. Two days later he
died in a clinic in Cairo. He was the twentieth victim of
the 'curse of the Pharaohs'.

What hitherto unknown powers are to be sought
behind these mysterious deaths, which are all officially
documented? Is it possible that forms of energy that are
still unidentified are activated as soon as anyone touches
the accursed remains?

Such a speculation acquires a fairly solid background
when we know that X-rays have only recently been used
to verify the presence of the most peculiar objects in
mummies that have lain in Cairo Museum since the beginning of the twentieth century. United Press International carried the report of the leader of an
archaeological group, James Harris from Ann Arbor,
Michigan. X-rays showed a *holy eye* on the left fore-
arm of Seti I (died 1343 B.C.). Thutmosis III (died
1447 B.C.) wore a technical gadget on his right fore-
arm which the investigators described as a *golden
brooch*. Queen Notmet wore four tiny statuettes and an
oval stone on her breasts. Previously it had been impossible to see anything of these adjuncts because the
mummies were covered with a thick black resinous
paste. X-rays disclosed these technical accessories for
the first time, although they are sure to appear in

archaeological literature as simple *ornaments*. According to James Harris, the Cairo authorities have not yet decided whether the precious, because hitherto unknown, finds can be removed from the mummies. It is devoutly to be hoped that this investigation can be continued with every kind of technical assistance. Perhaps science knows a solution to the puzzle of why small technical objects were placed in bodies whose insides had been removed. Perhaps they might even find out the secret behind the curse of the Pharaohs.

When the Pharaohs built their pyramids by the Nile, European history had not even begun. The first European 'buildings' consisted of megaliths, the most famous of which are at Stonehenge, England, a mecca for tourists from all over the world. Professor Alexander Thom, of Oxford, who has examined nearly 400 similar megalithic structures, explained to the newspaper *Welt am Sonntag*: 'Neolithic man had an almost incredible knowledge of astronomy and geometry.' Thom found out that some of these lay-outs were magnificent lunar observatories and that Palaeolithic men could 'work out results in advance that would need the help of a computer today'. Thus Neolithic men (4,000 to 1800 B.C.) could calculate the place where the moon would come out daily to the very slightest fraction of a second of arc. 3,000 years later this lost knowledge had to be rediscovered. These findings coincided with the reports by Professor Dr Rolf Müller, who proved that Stone Age men had laid out their megalithic monuments according to the constellations.

How is our book learning about Neolithic men, who learnt how to bore through stone in order to make stone axes, who flaked knives from stone or obsidian, who began to domesticate animals and practised agriculture for the first time with a few useful plants, who had just emerged from caves to build primitive dwellings, how is this book learning to be reconciled with the achievements of such a highly developed culture? Did the torpid cave dwellers have highly intelligent teachers? If so, where did they come from?

One continually comes across similar absurd contradictions. The banana, a delicious item of food, has been known in every tropical and subtropical region of the earth for many thousands of years. The Indian saga tells of the 'wonderful Kandali' (= banana bush) which the 'Manu', the loftiest spirits and protectors of mankind, brought to our planet from another star which was much further along the path of evolution than our earth. But a banana bush or banana tree simply does not exist! The banana is an annual plant which does not multiply by seeds, which it does not possess, but by suckers. Looked at in this light, the banana is a problem. It is found on even the most remote South Sea islands. How did this plant, which is so vital for the nourishment of mankind, originate? How did it make its way round the world, seeing that it has no seeds? Did the 'Manu', of whom the Indian saga tells, bring it with them from another star —as an all-round foodstuff?

The Uros, who live on reed islands in Lake Titicaca, Bolivia, claim that their people is older than that of the Incas, indeed, that they already existed before To Ti Tu, the father of heaven, who created the white men. The Uros swear black and blue that they were not men, for they had black blood and were alive when the earth still lay in darkness. *We are not as other men, for we came from another planet.* The few Uros who are still alive avoid any contact with the rest of the world. Proudly and stubbornly they defend their otherness as the heritage they brought with them from another planet.

Dr Alexander Marshack of Harvard's Peabody Museum of Archaeology examined several thousand bones, pieces of ivory and stones that all had the same patterns of dots, zig-zags and circles. Up to now it has been said that they were decorations. But Marshack says: 'They seem much more likely to be a form of writing which gives information about the phases of the moon and the constellations. The objects examined all date to a period from 10,000 to 30,000 B.C.'

What does this mean? Why did Stone Age men bother about astronomical representations? It is usually claimed that they had their hands full just to procure sufficient nourishment on endless hunting expeditions. Who instructed them in this work? Did someone advise them how to make these observations which were far above their 'level'? Were they making notes for an expected visit from the cosmos?

In the Temple of the Frescoes at Tulum, Mexico, archaeologists specialising in Mayan studies (Refield, Landa, Cogulludo, Roys) discovered bee gods—I'm almost ashamed to write it! The literature gives no information about the bee state and its hierarchy, it simply mentions that the 'Ah-Muzencab' were large bees, who ruled the others. The relief of the bee god bears not the slightest resemblance to a bee! It shows a being (certainly not a bee) lying on his stomach with arms apart and his forearms apparently supported on something. From his position one would be tempted to say that he was gripping steering controls in his hands. His feet, which are shod, seem to be working pedals. The bee god is surrounded with all kinds of technical gadgets that do not fit into any kind of beehive I have ever heard of! Is there anybody who is really prepared to accept this being as a bee god? If the artistically gifted Mayas had wanted, they would have conjured up the archaeologists a bee god which would have been much more convincing than this one. (Fig. 58.)

Fig. 58. The archaeologists call this strange being from Tulum, Mexico, a 'bee god'. An odd bee!

Fig. 59. This hideous creature with his two bombs is also classified as a 'bee god'.

There is another bee god in the Codex Tro-Cortesianus in Madrid. Once again a hideous creature, with arms apart, is lying on its stomach. On its back there are two classically shaped bombs, with broad bands and a fuse (fig. 59). Undoubtedly someone will say of the Madrid bee god that they are not bombs, but bee's wings! But when did bee's wings ever look like bombs? To be quite frank, I find it unintelligible that bee gods looking like technical monsters buzz their way through Mayan literature.

Some years ago Dr Carl Sagan put forward a proposal for making our neighbouring planet Venus inhabitable by having several tons of blue algae (Cyano Phyceae) blown into the hot Venusian atmosphere from space-ships. Blue algae are so resistant that great heat has no effect on them. They possess the quality of multiplying at

a fantastic speed and in enormous quantities and producing really vast amounts of oxygen. Sagan worked on
the premise that the oxygen would enrich the Venusian
atmosphere and cool down the surface of the planet, so
that with the rapid change storms and rain would make
the soil fertile. The astrophysicist Sagan seems to be on
the right track. The oldest demonstrable remains of
forms of life on earth were discovered in 3.5 milliard-
year-old sedimentary rock in the Transvaal, South
Africa. Their stage of development corresponds to that of
the blue algae living today! But 3.5 milliard years ago
there was no kind of organic life on our planet. The
palaeontologist H. D. Pflug of the University of Giessen
assumes that life is older than the earth!

One might well ask whether our blue planet was also
prepared for future life and settlement by the insufflation
of blue algae? And who initiated this process of biological transformation with that kind of biological planning?

For the past five years an American–Iranian team has
been excavating at Tepe Yahya, 155 miles south of
Kerman. Tepe Yahya was abandoned by its inhabitants
about the turn of the era. C. C. and Martha Lamberg-
Karlovsky, a husband and wife archaeological team,
found a large number of works of art made of bronze containing arsenic that were dated to at least 3500 B.C. The
material used in the Bronze Age—between the Neolithic
and the Iron Age—was made of copper, tin and lead.
Arsenic is found in nature in cobalt or united with other
elements in many minerals. It is very hard to imagine
how primitive men could have extracted arsenic for
making bronze alloys. But if an extension course was
held for the ancient bronze founders, we must look for
the masters who conducted it.

In the collection of the Springensguth family in San

Fig. 60. This vase from the private collection of the Springensguth family (San Salvador) shows an astronautess with all the attributes of her profession.

Salvador, El Salvador, I saw an old Mayan bowl (fig. 60), on which was shown a Mayan woman with the engine of a flying machine attached to her back. The figure has a very broad band round her stomach and the engine is fastened to it. A very similar figure decorates a vase in the Turkish Museum, Istanbul. In the American Museum, Madrid, there is a vase attributed to the Nazca culture. The only real difference in the representation on the $6\frac{3}{4}$ ins. high and 3 ins. wide vase is that this time it exhibits a mother goddess, an astronautess, who has a broad band slung round her stomach. Her shoulders and thighs have two straps round them. The goddess carries the inevitable engine for the flying machine on her back. This reminiscence of one-man flying machines, or rocket belts, seems to have left its traces nearly all over the world.

Professor Ruth Reyna was commissioned by the US space authorities to produce a report which was based on the interpretation of Indian Sanskrit texts. According to Dr Reyna, the Indians began spaceflights around 3000 B.C. in order to seek safety on Venus from the threat of a deluge. The Sanskrit texts were translated in the University of the Punjab.

The Chuwashen, a Tartaro-Finnish people in Russia who live on both banks of the Central Volga, still number about 1,500,000. Their everyday speech is an independent branch of Turkish. The Brasilian linguistic scholar Lubomir Zaphyrov, who specialises in Inca studies, has established that some 120 compound Inca words are still used today by the Chuwashen! They are precisely explained by about 170 simple Chuwashen words. Zaphyrov says that most of the words that have been preserved come from Inca mythology. Here are a few examples:

Viracocha = The good spirit from space

Kon Tiksi Illa Viracocha = Ruler of highest origin, radiant like lightning, the good spirit from space.

Chuvash = God out of the light

I will gladly give Professor Lubomir Zaphyrov's address to experts in the Chuwashen language who also understand Inca, and so that I do not have to send it all to them individually, here it is: Caixa Postal 6603, São Paulo, Brasil.

In 1972 the Unesco Courier gave an account of sensational finds made by the American archaeologist Manson Valentine and the underwater diver Dimitri Rebikoff immediately off the coasts of the islands of Bimini and Andros in the Bahamas. They came on submarine settlements with walls from 230 to 812 ft. long. The buildings, which lay more than 20 ft. under water, extended over an area of 38 sq. miles! There were parallel walls more than 2,000 ft. long. The weight of a single 16-ft.-long stone was 25 tons. Scholars from the University of Miami assign the settlement a date between 7000 and 10,000 B.C., even though measured by the C 14 method. Thus, according to currently accepted archaeological data, the Pyramids of Gizeh could not have been built nor the Sumerian Epic of Gilgamesh 'experienced' when these underwater buildings were constructed. Rebikoff is convinced that if these discoveries in the Bahamas were thoroughly investigated the reality would far exceed all the fantasy they can inspire today. Some of the foundations go about 250 ft. deep!

Has Atlantis been located in the Atlantic? I should not be surprised.

At a chemical congress in Los Angeles, Dr John Lynde Anderson of Chattanooga, Tennessee, explained that his experiments with the radio-active carbon isotope C 14 had produced deviations from the results which should be obtained according to the theory. To make sure he repeated his experiments with different equipment and on hundreds of organic objects, yet even on one and the same object the results were different.

Archaeologists still look on the C 14 method as the only canonised process for dating artefacts. How can people be so blind and stubborn?

North of Fairbanks, Alaska, and in the Yukon valley, deep-frozen woolly mammoths have been taken from deep in the ground during the last fifteen years when gold was being extracted with high-pressure pumps and excavators. The deep frozen stomachs contained leaves and grass which the animals had eaten. The young lay next to the old, the babies beside their mothers. Professor

Frank C. Hibben, an archaeologist from the University of New Mexico, says: 'Such quantities of animals cannot have died all at once in a natural way!' In fact, investigation showed that the animals must have died almost instantaneously and been deep frozen on the spot, otherwise they would have shown at least minimal signs of decomposition. In addition 1,766 jawbones and 4,838 metatarsal bones belonging to a single species of bison were found near Fairbanks.

Who organised this mass big game hunt here? And what cause brought about a change in climate that deep-froze animals that had just been grazing within a few hours?

When I rented a car outside the Taj Mahal Hotel in Bombay on 8 November, 1968, to travel south to Kanheri, near the Malabar coast, I was tempted by a tourist attraction. I wanted to see the 87 caves in the rock, also known as 'rock temples' in the guide-books. But when I walked about in the 48-ft.-high catacombs, I realised then (before I knew anything about the caves beneath Ecuador and Peru) that these caves blasted out of natural stone, mostly granite, that run to several storeys just like houses, must have been used for something quite different from religious ceremonies. One does not have to flee deep underground and sacrifice on altars in caves to gods who are worthy of adoration. No, cave systems like these were made by beings who sought protection from some prodigious threat. Plastic works of art depict the life of Shiva (Sanskrit: the believer) on anthracite-coloured walls that are often gleaming and iridescent. Shiva, image of destruction as well as salvation, forms the Indian trinity, the Trimurti, together with Brahman, the power which creates all worlds, and Vishnu, mentioned in the Veda as the 'penetrator'. As I traversed the gigantic halls I admired and marvelled at the ceilings, which were supported by pillars carved out of solid granite, and their masterly reliefs. Yet again I had to hear that the dating of the building period of these incredible structures is highly controversial, but that scholars of various disciplines assume that they were built by the Jains, representatives of a religion that originated before Buddhism, about 500 B.C. Once more one can only find the reasons for this titanic architectural feat in myths and legends. They tell that the sons of the gods, who were defeated in a war with the Kurus, the oldest people in western India, withdrew into these cave fortresses. Jains means 'victors' in Sanskrit. Were those apparently defeated in the war the victors in the end, because they had the sense to withdraw in time to caves prepared in advance? I assume that this was so, for Indian mythology emphasises that the caves were made in the rock so that people could protect themselves from the terrifying forces which threatened the living from the universe, from heaven.

In his book *When the Gods were Numerous*, Dr Bernhard Jacobi refers to 150 caves at Junnar on the Deccan plateau, the biggest group in India, to 27 caves at Ajanta and to 33 caves at Ellora.

I put forward a speculation for which I have given some support in this book.

1. In the unknown past a battle took place in the depths of the galaxy between intelligences similar to human beings.

2. The losers in this battle escaped in a spaceship.

3. As they knew the mentality of the victors, they set a 'trap', in that they did not land on the planet that was 'ideal' for their existence.

4. The losers chose the planet earth which was just acceptable in comparison with their home planet, but certainly did not offer ideal conditions. For many years

the losers continued to wear gasmasks in the *new* atmosphere in order to get used to the terrestrial air mixture (hence the helmets, trunks, breathing apparatus, etc., in cave drawings).

5. They burrowed deep into the earth and made the tunnel systems out of fear of their pursuers who were equipped with every kind of technical aid.

6. In order to deceive their opponents completely, they set up on the fifth planet of our solar system (i.e. not the earth) technical stations and transmitters which emitted coded reports.

7. The victors fell into the trap and believed the bluff. They brutally annihilated the fifth planet. It was destroyed by a gigantic explosion; parts of its substance shot through the planetoid belt. (A glance at the map of our solar system shows that there is an 'unnatural' gap of 300,000,000 miles between the *present-day* fourth and fifth planets, Mars and Jupiter. But the gap is not empty; hundreds and thousands of small lumps of stone, known collectively as the 'planetoid belt', are tumbling about in it. From time immemorial astronomers have been puzzling to explain how and why a planet can have 'exploded' between Mars and Jupiter. I venture to assert that planets do not 'explode' by themselves; someone makes them explode!)

8. The victors thought that the losers were destroyed. They withdrew their spaceships to their home planet.

9. Owing to the destruction of the fifth planet the gravitational balance in our solar system was temporarily thrown into confusion. The earth's axis moved a few degrees out of position. This resulted in tremendous inundations (there are legends of floods and deluges among peoples all over the world).

10. The losers emerged from their magnificently built catacombs and began to create intelligence on earth. Using their knowledge of the molecular biology, the

losers created man *in their image* from already existing
monkeys (the genetic code, sagas about the creation of
man, 'God's' promise to Abraham and others that their
descendants would be as numerous as the stars in
heaven, etc.).

11. The former losers, now absolute rulers and therefore *gods,* found that the progress and evolution of the
human race was too slow. They knew perfectly well that
the beings created by them were 'like gods', but they
wanted more rapid progress (Genesis i, 6: '. . . this they
begin to do: and now nothing will be restrained from
them, which they have imagined to do.'). The gods were
often hot-tempered in their impatience; they were quick
to punish and wipe out the malcontents and those who
did not follow the biological laws laid down, 'pour en-
courager les autres'. The gods had no 'moral' feelings
about such radical cleaning up operations for they felt
that they were responsible, as creators of men, for their
future development.

12. But men were afraid of the gods and their punitive
expeditions, especially once the gods were no longer first
generation gods, i.e. when they were their sons and
daughters to whom men believed they were already assi-
milated (proof: mythologies of the families of the gods).

13. Then whole groups of men began to dig themselves
underground hideouts out of fear of divine judgment.
Perhaps these groups of men still had tools available that
they had made under the gods' guidance—tools with
which they could perhaps work stone more easily than
archaeologists can imagine today.

14. It is a fact that today more and more gigantic
underground dwellings that are *not* identical to the
tunnel systems in Ecuador and Peru are being discovered
annually all over our globe. The subterranean human
cities which are constantly being discovered are obviously the work of many hands; they were not made with

sophisticated technical equipment such as the thermal drill. Such subterranean shelters, which men built out of fear of 'destruction from the cosmos', can be found, for example, at:

San Agustin, Colombia: underground sanctuaries with connecting passages;

Cholula, Mexico: underground temple with connecting passages. (Not to be confused with the passages stretching for kilometres installed by archaeologists.)

Derinkuyu, Anatolia, Turkey: underground cities with several-storeyed 'houses' and large assembly rooms.

15. If men, namely our ancestors, built safety bunkers underground by hand, with the expenditure of tremendous effort, they did not do so for pleasure, nor for protection against wild animals, nor to the glory of their religious ideals. Nor did they do so out of fear of some alien conquerors. Such excavations using simple tools and crude physical strength would have taken years. Alien conquerors would have had no difficulty in forcing these crazy defenders to surrender. They had only to sit down outside the cave entrances and starve the inmates to death.

16. I say that there was only one reason for the underground caves built by human hands and that was fear of attack from the air! But who could assail men from the air? Only those whom they knew by tradition, those gods who had once visited them long, long ago.

I know I am offering my head on a platter to every critic because of this daring speculation. But I am used to that by now.

Criticism and odium could not rain down on me more fiercely than they did after I quoted Ezekiel in *Chariots of the Gods?*. I must recapitulate!

It says in Ezekiel:

Fig. 61. At Derinkuyu, Anatolia (Turkey) there are underground cities with several storeys and rooms which hold as many as 60,000 men.

'Now it came to pass in the thirtieth year, in the fourth month, in the fifth day of the month, as I was among the captives by the river of Chebar, that the heavens were opened . . . And I looked, and, behold, a whirlwind came out of the north, a great cloud, and a fire infolding itself, and a brightness was about it, and out of the midst thereof as the colour of amber, out of the midst of the fire. Also out of the midst thereof came the likeness of four living creatures. And this was their appearance; they had the likeness of a man. And every one had four faces, and every one had four wings. And their feet were straight feet; and the sole of their feet was like the sole of a calf's foot: and they sparkled like the colour of burnished brass . . . Now as I beheld the living creatures, behold one wheel upon the earth by the living creatures . . . The appearance of the wheels and their work was like unto the colour of a beryl: and they four had one likeness: and their appearance and their work was as it were a wheel in the middle of a wheel. When they went, they went upon their four sides: and they turned not as they went. As for their rings, they were so high that they were dreadful: and their rings were full of eyes round about them four. And when the living creatures went, the wheels went by them: and when the living creatures were lifted up from the earth, the wheels were lifted up . . . "Son of man, stand upon thy feet, and I will speak unto thee.". . . and I heard behind me a voice of a great rushing . . . I heard also the noise of the wings of the living creatures that touched one another, and the noise of the wheels over against them, and a noise of a great rushing.'

Using this passage from Ezekiel, reproduced in abbreviated form here, I formulated some questions based on knowledge of current space travel technology. It was so obvious; it was so unmistakable. But the criticism and mockery I had to suffer for my modern exegesis!

On 28 March, 1972, I had a conversation with Joseph F. Blumrich in Huntsville, USA. Blumrich, an engineer born in Austria, has been working for NASA for 14 years. He is head of the department in which future space stations are planned on the drawing board and worked out in detail. For example, Blumrich was engaged on the construction of the last stage of Saturn V and is now planning the future orbital stations in which several astronauts will stay in space for weeks. In July 1972 Blumrich was awarded the NASA Exceptional Service Medal for his work on Saturn and Apollo—an honour received by very few NASA personnel.

'You have made a detailed study of the *visions* of the prophet Ezekiel in your spare time. First of all, how did a man in your position come to do this?'

'To put it quite bluntly—as a protest! I read your book *Chariots of the Gods?* with the superior attitude of a man who knew in advance that it was all rubbish. From the wealth of material supplied by you, I found, when I came to the description of the technical characteristics of Ezekiel's visions, a territory where I could join in the conversation, so to speak, as I have spent most of my life on the construction and planning of aircraft and rockets. So I got out a Bible to read the complete text, feeling sure that I would refute and annihilate you in a few minutes. You could not, you simply ought not to be right! After a careful perusal of the text, my conviction was rapidly undermined and the few minutes became a long period of intensive sparetime research, during which I worked out in detail and proved what I had found out in the first few hours.'

'Did you take into account the prophet Ezekiel as a person?'

'Naturally. From three points of view: in relation to his personality in general, his quality as a reporter and lastly, his participation in the events described. His personality influences the broad general evaluation of his report. As a reporter he possessed an outstanding gift of observation. As a participant he helps us to answer the question: was he the centre of the occurrence? Since he was not, the next question arises: why not?'

'Previously the encounters between God and man in

the Old Testament, which were always accompanied by secondary phenomena such as smoke, noise, fire, lightning and earthquakes, were called ideograms. Do you consider it possible after your Ezekiel studies that a meeting between the prophet and an alien intelligence can actually have taken place? If so, what indications do you base your findings on?'

'The answer to your first question is an unequivocal yes! But I don't agree with the word "indications". The general appearance of the spaceship described by Ezekiel can be winkled out of his account. Then an engineer can set aside his report and reconstruct a flying machine with the same characteristics. If he then shows that the result is not only technically possible, but also practical and well thought out in every respect, and moreover finds details and processes described in Ezekiel's account that tally perfectly with his own conclusion, you can no longer call them merely indications!'

'I know that you have written a book about your reflections and your calculations based on the prophet Ezekiel's data.* According to your calculations, was it possible to give data concerning comparative dimensions and technical know-how?'

'To my surprise it was possible to do so fairly accurately. Because of the vagueness in the prophet's original account, the mathematical side of the investigation was carried out parametrically, i.e. a series of variables were tried step by step. Naturally an extrapolation over and above the present-day state of technology that was partially based on theoretically known possibilities and partially on estimated values was also necessary. I found out that *Ezekiel's spaceship has very credible dimensions and belongs to a stage of technology which modern man will not reach for some decades!*'

* Blumrich's book will be published by Econ Verlag in the spring of 1973.

'I have no desire to pirate the results of your investigations before they are published, but I am naturally curious to know whether any questions are still left unanswered. Can you name two of them?'

'With pleasure. One concerns two rather similar possibilities. Does the account contain a mixture of visions *and* actual events or does it mention solely real observations? The second is what was the actual site of the temple to which Ezekiel was flown. Jerusalem cannot really be fitted into the two possibilities suggested. Obviously it would be of the highest importance to establish the actual site.'

'Mr Blumrich, do you realise that you're going to shock the Old Testament scholars—and others as well —with your logical calculations and reflections?'

'Undoubtedly a shock is unavoidable. Nevertheless, I hope to be able to reduce the duration of this shock to a minimum, because my book will contain all the technical data that I used for my calculations and reconstruction. It is all there in black and white. Anyone who doubts can check my work himself or have it checked. It doesn't take long and once it has been checked, the biggest shock should already have been overcome. There is no other way out. Naturally a longish time will have to elapse before my conclusions are adapted for use in different fields.'

For once my dearest wish has been fulfilled! An outstanding technician has taken my speculations with all the attendant evidence literally. I *want* my stimuli to thought to provoke protest—as in Blumrich's case. But I should also like those scholars who so often turn up their noses to take off their opaque spectacles and put on new clear ones in order—like Blumrich—to verify whether the fanciful Däniken does not sometimes offer paths at the end of which more real truth is to be found than on the old beaten tracks which still only go round in circles. *Errare humanum est!*

Sophocles (497–405 B.C.) makes Antigone say: 'Is it then so difficult, is it shameful to give up positions which, by tomorrow at the latest, will no longer be tenable?'

7: 'It'

Who or what created the universe?

Who or what installed the stars in outer space?

Who or what controls the 'lever' in cosmic space and amuses himself by making stars collide, suns explode and whole galaxies crash into one another?

Who or what 'breathed the breath of life' into the first form of life?

Who or what wanted intelligent life to come into being, wanted us to become the way we are?

If everything that is was created by the one and only God, then that God must be righteous, omnipotent and good, for everything is created according to his will.

Why does this almighty God let wars take place, let blood and tears flow?

If this God wants all men to 'serve' him, as the religions put it, why does he allow on a single planet 20,000 religions and sects who indulge in bloody conflicts with each other in his name?

How can the war material of two enemies be blessed for victory in the name of this God, who, religions say, was once a man and so must understand men in happiness and sorrow? Ought not the omniscient God to confer His blessing only on the party which is actually fighting in His name, at His bequest and will?

Why can knaves and rogues, assassins and false judges enjoy the same happiness as the good creatures under God's sun?

How can a wise and good God allow the rich to get richer and the poor poorer, when they are all His children?

What meaning has this one God decreed for intelligent life?

The molecular biologist Jacques Monod, Director of the Pasteur Institute, Paris, and Nobel Prize Winner in 1965, excited and upset the world of believers with his book *Chance and Necessity*, and even the atheistic left were outraged by Monod's thesis, because they suspected in it a philosophical inflation of biological facts into an *ersatz* religion.

In his book Monod names the three stages which made all life possible:

1. The formation of the mainly chemical components of living beings on earth: the nucleotides and the amino-acids. (Nucleotides are compounds of phosphoric acids, nucleic bases and carbohydrates which are found especially in the cell nuclei. Amino-acids are organic acids which are important in the building up of albumen.)

2. The formation, on the basis of these materials, of the first macromolecules capable of replication (macromolecules are those consisting of 1,000 or more atoms).

3. Around these infinitely repeatable structures is formed the teleonomic apparatus, a system that is complete in itself; it leads to the original cell.

Monod summarises the most recent work on molecular biology and genetics. Milliards of years ago certain simple carbon compounds (such as methane) entered the earth's atmosphere and the earth's crust. Later water and ammonia formed. From these simple compounds many substances originated, including nucleotides and amino-acids, which were finally combined into the first organism, the first cell, and consequently the first life, in the prebiotic primordial soup. In other words, that was a time when chemical and physical processes were not yet dependent on the presence of living beings. (*Gods from Outer Space.*) The 'short step' to the evolution of *homo sapiens* ostensibly comes into the theory of evolution in a peaceful development without revolutionary intervention.

The core of Monod's thesis is that the decisive event of life coming into being took place *once and once only*. Monod says: 'Man knows at last that he is alone in the indifferent illimitable universe, from which he emerged by chance. Nothing about his fate and his duty was ever decreed.'

Life as a winner of nature's lottery? Although the atheistic professor's ideas may have an impeccable scientific foundation, the decisive question still remains unanswered. What primordial force prepared the chemical substances for the coming into being of life? Whence came the ingredients for the primordial soup on which the first life swam like the circles of fat on top of consommé?

Out of the atmosphere, of course, answers science. But that answer does not satisfy me. Like a curious child I ask: where did the atmosphere come from? From the envelope of the cooling earth, my son. And where did the earth come from? It is a part of the sun, my son. And the sun? It is a part of the Milky Way, my son. Where does the Milky Way come from? It is part of all the other Milky Ways in the universe, my son. And where do those Milky Ways come from? There are only theories about that, my son.

Professor Georges Lemaître, physicist and mathematician from Brussels, introduced a phenomenal idea into the endless discussions about the origin of all worlds. Milliards of years ago all the matter in the universe was compressed into a single original atom, a heavy mass of matter, the cohesion of which pressed permanently against its nucleus. The incredible forces involved added and multiplied so that the lump of matter exploded. Splintered into many, many milliards of pieces, the bits of matter assembled into infinitely numerous galaxies over a long period of consolidation. The Russian physicist George Gamow (1904–), who came to the University of Michigan by way of Paris and London, is known in the scientific world for his knack of inventing catch phrases. He introduced into scientific literature the handy phrase 'big bang' to describe the theory which was accepted as most probable in scientific circles that the origin of all worlds and therefore of life was due to a gigantic explosion. It is completely credible that the creation began with a 'big bang'.

The big bang theory has the advantage over all the other theories of being susceptible of *proof* by what is known as the Doppler effect. In 1842, Professor Christian Doppler (1803–1853), an Austrian physicist, discovered the effect that applies to all kinds of waves, including light and sound. 'The Doppler effect' consists in an alteration of the pitch of sound when the source of sound or the listener moves. If their distance apart increases, the tone grows deeper, if it decreases, it rises. This phenomenon can be observed when a whistling locomotive approaches or recedes. In light waves the spectrum shifts towards blue if the source of light moves towards the observer, and towards red if the source of light moves away from him. The velocity of the movement of all stars can be measured by the Doppler effect, because it has been proved that the stars in all galaxies have the same chemical consistencies and often the same physical conditions as the stars in our Milky Way.

On the basis of this established fact the astrophysicist Edwin Powell Hubble (1889–1953) discovered during his work on cosmic mist and stellar systems at the Mount Wilson Observatory that the shift of the galaxies to red increased as their distance away from us increased.

Professor Hannes Alfvén, Professor of Plasma Physics at the Royal Technical College in Stockholm, says: 'The galaxies are moving away from us at speeds that are proportional to their distances from us.' The frequency of light becomes one per cent smaller if the source of light moves away from us at a speed of one per cent of the speed of light (= 186,000 miles per second). The reader should imagine a coloured children's balloon that has not yet been blown up. If red dots are added to the deflated balloon and it is then blown up, each of the red dots moves away from the others at a proportional speed, because every dot is pulled faster and further from the others the larger the balloon gets. Obviously one can work out when all the dots were together at one centre from the speed given by the distances of the dots from one another and from the directions in which they move.

The age of the universe has been calculated by the red shift method, giving an age of six to ten milliard years. Just as everyone had agreed to this estimate, George Abell, Head of the Astronomical Department of the University of California, spoke up in November, 1971, and said: 'You're wrong, gentlemen. After thirteen years of observing eight widely separated galaxies I can prove that the universe is twice as old as was previously thought.'

Big bang!

The universe is no lady who can be insulted by making her older than she is. And it makes no difference to me whether six, ten or twenty milliard years have passed since the original big bang. Its *age* says nothing about the *origin of the first life*. But no matter when the fireworks took place, something must have been present before them. The explosion of the primordial atom may explain the origin of the galaxies with milliards and milliards of stars. Scientists of all disciplines and even philosophers may penetrate ever deeper into the secret of the atom as the beginning of all things. Atheists may deny with ever increasing vehemence the existence of a power whom for want of a better word we call 'God'. In the beginning there was a creation.

If the matter composing all the stars comes from the primordial atom, it is only logical that the stars in all the galaxies are made of the same stuff, i.e. consist of the same elements. Either the big bang theory can be proved by the red shift, in which case all matter was originally compressed into one lump, or there was no big bang and then nothing can be deduced from the red shift or the Doppler effect.

Actually, precisely during the last two years, more and more amino-acids and complexes of molecular compounds have been established in extraterrestrial matter. On 29 October, 1971, the geologists Gösta Vollin and David B. Ericson of Columbia University, New York, announced in *Nature* that during laboratory experiments they had succeeded in producing amino-acids by irradiating a mixture of four kinds of matter that demonstrably exist in the universe. Almost simultaneously research workers at the Radio-astronomical Observatory of Green Bank, West Virginia, reported that in gas cloud B2 in the constellation of Sagittarius they had found a substance that contains all the prerequisites for the origination of life. It was cyano-azethylene, the most complicated chemical compound that it has so far been possible to demonstrate in interstellar space. Molecules of hydrogen, carbon monoxide, ammonia, water, hydrocyanide, formaldehyde, formic acid, methyl alcohol and a series of carbohydrates have been shown to exist in the universe, as have amino-acids in meteorites and lunar rocks. In October 1971 NASA scientists reported that they could prove the existence of 17(!) amino-acids—including ones found as protein builders in all terrestrial organisms—in the Murchinson and Murray meteorites (named after the sites in South Australia). The University of Miami found two free protein-building amino-acids, glycin and alanin, in lunar rocks brought back by the crew of Apollo XI.

Actually man, who so dislikes being alone, ought to be very happy about these scientific proofs which assure him that he is not alone in the cosmos, and that on the contrary probably lots of clever playfellows are waiting there for him to pick up the traces of their former visits that they left behind. For according to the present state of knowledge we should accept the following facts:

All matter in the universe was originally united in one primordial atom.

The chemical prerequisites for life exist on other stars in our galaxy.

But where is there room for the 'good God' in this fantastic theoretical structure erected by science?

The personification of the force that *must* have existed *before* the original big bang as God, and the conceptions of this kindly old man produced for the faithful by the catechists simply blindfold us.

The original prodigious force which existed before the beginning of all being was a neutrum. IT existed before the big bang. IT unleashed the great destruction. IT caused all the worlds in the universe to originate from the explosion. IT, incorporeal primordial force, the decisive primordial command, became matter and IT knew the result of the great explosion. IT wanted to reach the stage of lived experience.

In the course of countless discussions I have tried to express this concept of mine by a highly simplified example. *Terrible simplificateur!*

I suggested that one should imagine a computer that works with 100 milliard thought units (bits in computer jargon). It would have a 'personal consciousness', as

Professor Michie, of Edinburgh University, who developed the prototype of the first *thinking* computer, called it. The computer's personal consciousness is tightly attached to the complicated machinery with its milliards of circuits. If this computer exploded, its 'personal consciousness' would be destroyed, had not the intelligent computer magnetised all its milliards of bits before the explosion. The explosion takes place. 100 milliard bits shoot off in all directions at various speeds depending on their size. The originally centralised computer consciousness no longer exists, but the clever self-destroyer had programmed the future *after* the explosion. All the magnetic bits with their separate information will meet again some time at the centre of the explosion. Once it is back, each bit adds a new factor, personal *experience,* to the original 'personal consciousness' of the great machine. From the moment of the explosion to the moment of return no 'bit' knew that it was a minute part of a larger consciousness and was now going to be so again. If an individual bit with its minimal thinking capacity had been able to ask 'What is the sense and purpose of my headlong journey?' or 'Who created me, where do I come from?', it would have received no answer. Nevertheless, it was the beginning and end of an act, a kind of 'creation' of consciousness multiplied by the factor 'experience'. Only right at the end, at Teilhard de Chardin's (1881–1955) Omega-point, shall we know again that we unite in ourselves the cause and result of creation.

It seems to me to be an incontrovertible idea that IT, synonym for the concept God, *must* have existed *before* the original big bang. St John the Divine, who shows in Revelations that he had access to secret texts, described the origin of all being:

'In the beginning was the Word, and the Word was with God, and the Word was God.

All things were made by him; and without him was not anything made that was made.'

That would all be logical if the concept God had not been loaded in the course of two thousand years with accretions which provide us with a story of the creation suitable for children and savages, but which prevent us from getting to the heart of the real mystery of the creation. But if the phenomenon IT (God) decided to transform itself into matter, then IT is the creation and at the same time a product of its creation. What does Professor D. L. Pieper of Stanford University say? 'Panic fear of a mistake is death to any form of progress. Love of truth is its letter of safe conduct.'

Like the computer bits we find ourselves again in a unity. We are parts, minute parts, of the IT, which will find their way back to the infinite cosmological community. All theories, all philosophies torture themselves with the questions 'why' and 'whence'. 'Knowledge,' writes the theologian Professor Puccetti, 'does not necessarily have to be won on scientific paths and in fact no so-called religious truth of importance has ever been arrived at in this way.'

On the threshold of the third millennium of our era the world is split into five great rival religions and thousands of fanatical sects.

With great certainty technology will enable us to establish communications with alien intelligences in the cosmos.

How do we imagine them?

As Catholics? As Protestants? As Lutherans? As Mormons? As Muslims? As Buddhists? As Hindus? As Greek Orthodox?

Shall we be looked on by an alien intelligence as mentally deficient because we never switch on the light on Saturday? (Orthodox Jews.) Because we do not eat pork? (Mohammedans and Jews.) Because we look on skinny cows and fat rats as sacred? (Hindus and kindred religions.) Or because we nailed our almighty God to the cross in gruesome fashion?

I suspect that with the step into the interstellar third millennium the end of terrestrial polytheism will inevitably come.

With the assumption that we are all parts of the mighty IT God no longer has to be simultaneously good and bad in some inconceivable way; He is no longer responsible for sorrow and happiness, for ordeals and acts of providence. We ourselves have the positive and negative powers within us, because we come from the IT that always was.

I cannot avoid this question of the IT, or God, in more inflated language, nor do I want to, because I am convinced that religions with their countless gods hinder progress. How often have religions and sects, each of them vowed to one god, been the cause of wars, misery and abominations! And if their insight does not improve, they will be a contributing cause of the end of human existence.

The systems analyst Jay W. Forrester of the Massachusetts Institute of Technology has made an extremely detailed study of the rates of human growth and its consequences. *The Limits of Growth* (May, 1972) is the title of the book in which Professor Dennis Meadows confronted the world with the terrifying future prospects based on Forrester's calculations. The number of human beings grows daily, hourly. A human flood is inundating our planet. All men need food, clothing, housing. All men produce refuse and excrement, increase nitrogen. More agricultural land and more raw materials are needed than are available on our planet. Like the metastasis of a cancerlike tumour the earth's surface is overgrown with towns and settlements. Yet if man roots up jungles and forests in his dire necessity, he is committing suicide. He is destroying the sources of oxygen. The elixir of life, water, is no longer sufficient even if the oceans and the volume of the polar ice are taken into account. The scientists warn us that the earth will perish before the year 2100.

There is only one solution to this problem: immediate and rigorous birth control. The leaders of large and small religious communities oppose this as if they had come to a global cartel agreement. Every community counts its sheep and more sheep mean more power, even if the attendant misery cannot truthfully be represented as willed by God. What is allowed to happen here in God's name is power politics played with the most miserable of creatures, it is a crime against humanity. Against men made in God's image?

Ought not man to conceive of himself as an essential part of the cosmos at last? Starting from this position he would acquire a more balanced sense of his own importance, he could hold on to his world as home and at the same time make a more daring reach for the stars. The future will bring space travel—the moon landings were only a beginning—because we shall need raw materials and also space. But space travel will also bring with it, with a probability bordering on certainty, the encounter with the 'lord from the other star'.

This encounter has no place in the doctrines of the 20,000 religions and sects, for the faithful sheep, man, must remain the summit of creation. But what if intelligent beings far superior to us exist on other planets without the benefit of the divine act of creation? Is it so difficult to say goodbye to familiar and well-loved fairy stories?

In a devilishly clever way 'they' try to sabotage space travel and its goal. 'They' warn against the results of research aimed at this goal. This way of thinking is so insidious that many clever critics of plans for space travel no longer realise who is guiding their pen when they put forward their arguments.

What are we to do then?

Are we to blow up the temples, demolish the churches? Certainly not.

In all the places where men gather together to praise the creator, they feel a beneficent strengthening togetherness. As if roused by the note of a tuning fork, the shared sense of something transcendent echoes silently through the interior. Temples and churches are places for contemplation, spaces for the communal praise of the indefinable, of IT, which for want of a better word we have learnt to call God. The places of assembly are necessary, but the rest is superfluous.

Bibliography

ALFVÉN, HANNES, *Worlds–antiworlds*, W. H. Freeman & Co., 1966.

ALLEN, T., *Wesen, die noch niemand sah*, Bergisch Gladbach, 1966.

ANDERS, FERDINAND, *Das Pantheon der Maya*, Graz, 1963.

ANDREAS, P. and ADAMS, G., *Between Heaven and Earth*, Verry, Lawrence, Inc., 1967.

ARDREY, ROBERT, *African Genesis*, Atheneum, 1961.

BANCO DE LA REPUBLICA, *Museo del Oro*, Bogotá, 1968.

BARRETO, FELICITAS, *Danzas Indigenas del Brasil*, Mexico, 1960.

BASS, GEORGE F., *Archaeology under Water*, Penguin, 1972.

BAUDIN, LOUIS, *Socialist Empire: Incas of Peru*, Van Nostrand–Reinhold Co., 1961.

BECK, C. H., *Menschenzüchtung*, Munich, 1969.

BERTELSMANN, *Hausatlas*, Gütersloh, 1960.

BIEDERMANN, HANS, *Altmexicos heilige Bücher*, Graz, 1970.

BLAVATSKY, H. P., *The Secret Doctrine*, Vols. I–IV, Theosophical Publishing Co., London, 1888.

BLÜHEL, KURT, *Projekt Übermensch*, Bern-Stuttgart, 1971.

BOGEN, HANS J., *Biology for the Modern Mind*, Macmillan, 1969.

BOSCHKE, F. L., *Erde von anderen Sternen*, Düsseldorf, 1965.

BOSCHKE, F. L., *Die Herkunft des Lebens*, Düsseldorf, 1970.

BÖTTCHER, HELMUTH M., *Die grosse Mutter*, Düsseldorf, 1968.

BRAGIN, A. P., *The Shadow of Atlantis*, Rider & Co., 1938.

BRANCO, RENATO CASTELO, *Pre-Historia Brasileira*, São Paulo, 1972.

BRENTJES, B., *African Rock Art*, Clarkson N. Potter, 1970.

BREUER, HANS, *Columbus was Chinese*, Herder & Herder, 1972.

BRION, MARCEL, *Die frühen Kulturen der Welt*, Cologne, 1964.

BRUCKNER, WINFRIED, *Spuren ins All*, Volksbuchverlag, undated.

BUCK, PETER, *Vikings of the Pacific*, Univ. of Chicago Press, 1959.

BUTLAR, JOH. VON, *Schneller als das Licht*, Düsseldorf–Vienna, 1972.

CATHIE, B. L., *Harmonic 695*, Wellington, 1971.

CERAM, C. W., *The First American*, New American Library, 1972.

CHARROUX, ROBERT, *Le livre des secrets trahis*, Robert Laffont, Paris, 1965.

CHARROUX, ROBERT, *Forgotten Worlds*, Walker & Co., 1973.

CHARROUX, ROBERT, *Mysterious Unknown*, Wehman Brothers, 1971.

CHARROUX, ROBERT, *Die Meister der Welt*, Düsseldorf, 1972.

CHEN CHIH-PING, *Chinese History*, Taipeh, undated.

CHIANG FU-TSUNG, *Masterworks of Chinese Bronze in the National Palace Museum*, Taipeh, 1969.

CHIANG FU-TSUNG, *The Origin and Development of the National Palace Museum*, Taipeh, undated.

CODEX TRO-CORTESIANUS, The American Museum, Madrid.

COMFORT, ALEX and others, *The Biological Future of Man*, Routledge, 1969.

CORDAN, WOLFGANG, *Das Buch des Rates, Mythos und Geschichte der Maya*, Düsseldorf, 1962.

COVARRUBIAS, M., *Indian Art of Mexico and Central America*, Alfred A. Knopf, 1957.

CRAMP, LEONARD G., *Piece for a Jig-saw*, Somerton Publishing Co., Cowes, I.O.W., 1966.

DANIELSSON, B., *Forgotten Islands of the South Seas*, George Allen & Unwin, 1957.

DÄNIKEN, ERICH VON, *Chariots of the Gods?*, G. P. Putnam's Sons, 1970.

DÄNIKEN, ERICH VON, *Gods from Outer Space*, G. P. Putnam's Sons, 1971.

DARLINGTON, C. D., *The Evolution of Man and Society*, Simon and Schuster, 1970.

DEUEL, LEO, *Flights into Yesterday*, St. Martin's Press, 1969.

DISSELHOFF, H. D., *Gott muss Peruaner sein*, Wiesbaden, 1956.

EHRENREICH, PAUL, *Die Mythen und Legenden der südamerikanischen Urvölker*, Berlin, 1905.

EINSTEIN, A., *The Meaning of Relativity*, Dover, 1924.

EISELEY, LOREN, *Darwin's Century, Evolution and the Men Who Discovered It*, Doubleday, 1958.

EISSFELDT, OTTO, *The Old Testament*, Harper & Row, 1965.

ELIADE, MIRCEA, *The Myth of the Eternal Return*, Routledge & Kegan Paul, 1955.

ELSÄSSER, HANS and others, *Sind wir allein im Kosmos?*, Munich, 1970.

EUGSTER, J., *Die Forschung nach ausserirdischem Leben*, Zurich, 1969.

FERREIRA, MANOEL RODRIGUES, *O misterio do ouro dos martirios*, São Paulo, 1960.

FRISCHAUER, P., *Es steht geschrieben*, Munich, 1967.

FUCHS, WILHELM, *Formeln zur Macht*, Stuttgart, 1965.

GAMOW, GEORGE, *Biography of the Earth*, Viking Press, 1959.

GAMOW, GEORGE, *A Planet called Earth*, Viking Press, 1963.

GIRO, ELVIRA, *Rivelazioni spirituali cosmiche nella chiesa universale giurisdavidica della SS. ma Trinita*, Rome, 1968.

GOMEZ, L. D., *San Agustin* (Instituto colombiano de antropologia), Bogotá, 1963.

GOOD-IRVING, JOHN, *Phantasie in der Wissenschaft*, Düsseldorf, 1965.

GRAND PALAIS, *Arts Mayas du Guatemala*, Paris, 1968.

HABER, HEINZ, *Our Blue Planet*, Scribner's, 1972.

HAGEN, VICTOR VON, *World of the Maya*, New American Library, 1965.

HAMBRUCH, PAUL, *Ponape, Ergebnisse der Südsee-Expedition*, Berlin, 1936.

HAPGOOD, CH. H. *Maps of the Ancient Sea Kings*, Chilton Books, 1971.

HEITMANN, KARL E., *Die Urzeitjäger im technischen Paradies*, Düsseldorf, 1962.

HERODOTUS (Trans. G. Rawlinson), *The Histories of Herodotus*, Dutton, 1964.

HERTEL, J., *The Panchatranta*, Krishna Press, undated.

HEYERDAHL, THOR, *Aku-Aku*, Rand McNally & Co., 1958.

HOENN, K., *Sumerische und akkadische Hymnen und Gebete*, Zurich/Stuttgart, 1953.

HONORÉ, PIERRE, *Das Buch der Altsteinzeit*, Düsseldorf, 1967.

HÜBNER, PAUL, *Vom ersten Menschen wird erzählt*, Düsseldorf, 1969.

JACOBI, BERNHARD, *Als die Götter zahlreich waren*, Frankfurt, 1968.

JACOBI, CLAUS, *Die menschliche Springflut*, Berlin, 1969.

KHUON, ERNST VON, *Waren die Gotter Astronauten?*, Düsseldorf, 1970.

KNAURS, *Welt-Atlas*, Munich, 1955.

KNAURS, *Weltgeschichte*, Munich, 1959.

KOHLENBERG, KARL F., *Enträtselte Vorzeit*, Munich, 1970.

KOLOSIMO, PETER, *Not of this World*, Souvenir Press, 1970.

KOLOSIMO, PETER, *Sie kamen von einem anderen Stern*, Wiesbaden, 1969.

KOLOSIMO, PETER, *Viele Dinge zwischen Himmel und Erde*, Wiesbaden, 1970.

KOLOSIMO, PETER, *Woher wir kommen,* Wiesbaden, 1972.
KRAMER, S. N., *History Begins at Sumer,* Doubleday, 1959.
KRASSA, PETER, *Gott kam von den Sternen,* Vienna, 1969.
KRICKEBERG, WALTER, *Märchen der Azteken und Inka,* Jena, 1928.
KRICKEBERG, WALTER, *Die Religion des alten Amerika,* Stuttgart, 1952.
KÜHN, H., *Wenn Steine reden,* Wiesbaden, 1966.
KUNSTGEWERBEMUSEUM DER STADT ZÜRICH, *Felsritzungen im Val Camonica,* Zurich, 1970.
LAVONDÈS, ANNE, *Art ancien de Tahiti* (Société des Océanistes), Paris, undated.
LEHNER, E. and J., *Lore and Lure of Outer Space,* New York, 1964.
LEON-PORTILLA, MIGUEL, *The Broken Spears. The Aztec Account of the Conquest of Mexico,* Beacon Press, 1962.
LHOTE, HENRI, *Die Felsbilder der Sahara,* Zettner, 1958.
LIEBENFELS, LANZ J., VON, *Bibliomystikon,* Pforzheim, 1930.
LINDNER, HELMUT, *Physik im Kosmos,* Cologne, 1971.
LÖBSACK, THEO, *Die Biologie und der liebe Gott,* Munich, 1968.
LUCAS, HEINZ, *Japanische Kultmasken,* Kassel, 1965.
LUKIAN, *Zum Mond und darüber hinaus,* Zurich, 1967.
MAERTH, OSCAR KISS, *Der Anfang war das Ende,* Düsseldorf, 1971.
MARINS, FRANCISCO, *The Mystery of the Gold Mines,* U.L.P., 1961.
MATSCHOSS, CONRAD, *Beiträge zur Geschichte der Technik und Industrie* (Jahrbuch des Vereins deutscher Ingenieure), Berlin, 1928.
MAZIÈRE, FRANCIS, *Mysteries of Easter Island,* Collins, 1969.
McLUHAN, MARSHALL and FIORE, QUENTIN, *War and Peace in the Global Village,* Bantam Books, 1969.
MEISSNER, B., *Babylonien und Assyrien,* Winter, 1925.

MELHEDEGARD, FREDE, *Tut-ankh-amon er vagnet*, Fredericia, 1970.

MELLAART, JAMES, *Çatal Hüyük: Aneolithic Town in Anatolia*, McGraw-Hill, 1967.

METZGER, HENRI (Trans. J. Hogarth), *Anatolia II*, Barrie & Rockliff, 1969.

MINISTERIO DA AGRICULTURA, *Paraque national de sete cidades*, Piaui, 1971.

MONOD, JACQUES, *Chance and Necessity*, Random House, 1972.

MOORE, PATRICK, *Atlas of the Universe*, Mitchell Beazley & George Philip, 1970.

MORICZ, JUAN, *El origen americano de pueblos europeos*, Guayaquil, 1968.

MÜLLER, ROLF, *Der Himmel über dem Menschen der Steinzeit*, Heidelberg, 1970.

MUSEO DE ETNOLOGIA Y ANTROPOLOGIA, *Publicaciones*, Santiago de Chile, 1922.

NATIONAL MUSEUM OF HISTORY, *4,000 Years of Chinese Art*, Taipeh, undated.

NATIONAL PALACE MUSEUM, *Chinese Cultural Art Treasures*, Taipeh, 1971.

NEWMAN, ALFRED K., *Who are the Maoris?*, Whitcombe & Tombs: Christchurch, N.Z., 1913.

OLIVEIRA, DECIO RUFINO DE, *Fenomenos parapsicologicos e energia consciente*, São Paulo, 1969.

OSTEN-SACKEN, P. V. Der, *Wanderer durch Raum und Zeit*, Stuttgart, 1965.

OSTRANDER, SHEILA-LYNN, SCHROEDER, *Psychic Discoveries Behind the Iron Curtain*, Prentice-Hall, 1970.

PAASONEN, HEIKKI, *Gebräuche und Volksdichtung der Tschuwassen*, Helsinki, 1949.

PARROT, ANDRÉ, *Sumerian Art*, New American Library, undated.

PARROT, ANDRÉ, *Arts of Assyria*, George Braziller, undated.

PAUWELS, L. and BERGIER, J., *Morning of the Magicians*, Stein & Day, 1964.

PAUWELS, L. and BERGIER, J., *Impossible Possibilities*, Stein & Day, 1971.

PAUWELS, L. and BERGIER, J., *The Eternal Man*, Souvenir Press, 1972.

PHILBECK, MAYNARD, *The Search for the Sun People*, Washington, D.C., 1968.

PHILBERTH, BERNHARD, *Christliche Prophetie und Nuklearenergie*, Zurich, 1967.

PHILIP, BROTHER, *Secret of the Andes*, Wehman Brothers, 1961.

PLOETZ, KARL, *Epitome of History*, Finch Press, 1925.

POINTER, JOSEF, *Das Weltraum-Dilemma*, Düsseldorf, 1971.

PRESCOTT, WILLIAM H., *History of the Conquest of Peru*, E. P. Dutton, 1969.

PUCCETTI, ROLAND, *Persons. A Study of Possible Moral Agents in the Universe*, Macmillan, 1968.

READER'S DIGEST, *Great World Atlas*, Funk & Wagnalls Co., 1968.

REICHE, M., *Geheimnis der Wüste*, Stuttgart, undated.

RITTLINGER, HERBERT, *Der masslose Ozean*, Stuttgart, undated.

ROCHOLL-ROGGERSDORF, *Das seltsame Leben des Erich von Däniken*, Düsseldorf, 1970.

ROSENFELD, ALBERT, *Die zweite Schöpfung*, Düsseldorf, 1970.

RÜEGG, W., *Die ägyptische Götterwelt*, Zurich/Stuttgart, 1959.

SAHER, P. J., *Symbole* (Die magische Geheimsprache der Poesie), Ratingen, 1968.

SÄNGER-BREDT, IRENE, *Spuren der Vorzeit*, Düsseldorf, 1972.

SÄNGER-BREDT, IRENE, *Ungelöste Rätsel der Schöpfung*, Düsseldorf, 1971.

SAURAT, DENIS, *Atlantis and the Giants*, Faber & Faber, 1957.

SCHIRMBECK, HEINRICH, *Ihr werdet sein wie die Götter*, Düsseldorf, 1966.

SCHMIDT, ULRICH, *Treppen der Götter, Zeichen der Macht*, Düsseldorf, 1970.

SCHRADER, HERBERT L., *Der Mensch wird umgebaut*, Frankfurt, 1970.

SCHRADER, HERBERT L., *Der achte Tag der Schöpfung*, Berlin, 1964.

SCHWENNHAGEN, LUDWIG, *Antiga historia do Brasil*, Rio de Janeiro, 1970.

SEKI, KEIGO, *Folktales of Japan*, University of Chicago Press, 1963.

SETE, K., *Das ägyptische Totenbuch*, Leipzig, 1931.

SHKLOVSKY, J. S. and SAGAN, C., *Intelligent Life in the Universe*, San Francisco, 1966.

SMITH, PERCY S., *Hawaiki*, Whitcombe & Tombs, 1910.

STEIN, WERNER, *Kultur-Fahrplan*, Gütersloh, 1970.

STEINBUCH, KARL, *Die informierte Gesellschaft*, Stuttgart, 1968.

STERNEDER, HANS, *Also spricht die Cheopspyramide*, Freiburg i. Br., 1968.

STINGL, MILOSLAV, DR., *In versunkenen Mayastädten*, Leipzig, 1971.

STINGL, MILOSLAV, DR., *Ostrovy lidojedu*, Prague, 1970.

STODDARD, THEODORE L., *Indians of Brazil in the Twentieth Century*, Washington, D.C., 1967.

STUCKEN, EDUARD, *Polynesisches Sprachgut in Amerika und Sumer*, Leipzig, 1927.

SULLIVAN, NAVIN, *Message of the Genes*, Basic Books, 1967.

TAYLOR, GORDON RATTRAY, *The Biological Time-bomb*, Norton, 1968.

TEILHARD DE CHARDIN, PIERRE, *The Future of Man*, Harper & Row, 1969.

TEILHARD DE CHARDIN, PIERRE, *Man's Place in Nature*, Harper & Row, 1966.

TEILHARD DE CHARDIN, PIERRE, *The Phenomenon of Man*, Harper & Row, 1959.

TOBISCH, O. OSWALD, *Kult Symbol Schrift*, Baden-Baden, 1963.

TOFFLER, ALVIN, *Future Shock*, Random House, 1970.

TOMAS, ANDREW, *We Are Not the First*, G. P. Putnam's Sons, 1971.

TREGEAR, EDWARD, *The Maori Race*, Dawson & Son, 1905.

UMSCHAU VERLAG, *Die biologische Zukunft des Menschen*, Frankfurt am Main, 1971.

VALLE, JACQUES and JANINE, *Challenge to Science*, Chicago, 1966.

VESTENBRUGG, RUDOLF ELMAYER, *Eingriffe aus dem Kosmos*, Freiburg i. Br., 1971.

VILLAS BOAS, O. and C., *Xingu*, Souvenir Press, 1973.

WAISBARD, SOMONE, *Masks, Mummies and Magicians: Inca Civilization in Peru*, Albert Saifer, undated.

WATERS, FRANK, *Book of the Hopi*, New York, 1963.

WATSON, JAMES D., *The Double Helix*, Atheneum, 1968.

WEDEMEYER, INGE VON, *Sonnengott und Sonnenmenschen*, Tübingen, 1970.

WEIDENREICH, F., *Apes, Giants and Man*, Univ. of Chicago Press: Cambridge U.P., 1946.

WHITE, JOHN, *Ancient History of the Maori*, Vols. I–III, Sampson Low, Marston & Co., 1889.

WIESNER, JOSEPH, *Histoire de l'art*, Paris, undated.

General Index

Index of Names

Get these fascinating books from your nearest bookstore or directly from:
Adventures Unlimited Press
www.adventuresunlimitedpress.com

TAYOS GOLD: The Archives of Atlantis
By Stan Hall

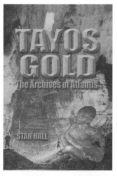

In 1976, Scottish engineer Hall organized a landmark expedition to Ecuador, involving joint Special Forces and astronaut professor Neil Armstrong. Hall was driven by curiosity about Erich von Däniken's report of a Metal Library allegedly found in the caves by investigator Juan Moricz in the mid-1960s and began an odyssey into the heart of global enigmas: the origins of mankind, Atlantis, and the entrance to the Metal Library along the Pastaza River in Ecuador. Chapters include: Juan Moricz-Magyar Extraordinary; Egyptian Tablets of the Mormons; Ecuador: Cradle of Civilization; The Triangle of the Shell, Tunnels Below the Andes; Neil Armstrong: Second Small Step; Into the Tayos Caves; Treasure of the Incas; Explorers Percy Fawcett and George M. Dyott; Valverde's Treasure; Tayos Treasure: Analysis and Location; more.
246 pages. 6x9 Paperback. Illustrated. $18.95. Code: TAYG

THE ENIGMA OF CRANIAL DEFORMATION
Elongated Skulls of the Ancients
By David Hatcher Childress and Brien Foerster

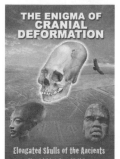

In a book filled with over a hundred astonishing photos and a color photo section, Childress and Foerster take us to Peru, Bolivia, Egypt, Malta, China, Mexico and other places in search of strange elongated skulls and other cranial deformation. The puzzle of why diverse ancient people—even on remote Pacific Islands—would use head-binding to create elongated heads is mystifying. Where did they even get this idea? Did some people naturally look this way—with long narrow heads? Were they some alien race? Were they an elite race that roamed the entire planet? Why do anthropologists rarely talk about cranial deformation and know so little about it? Color Section.
250 Pages. 6x9 Paperback. Illustrated. $19.95. Code: ECD

ARK OF GOD
The Incredible Power of the Ark of the Covenant
By David Hatcher Childress

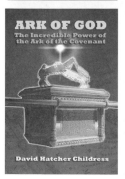

Childress takes us on an incredible journey in search of the truth about (and science behind) the fantastic biblical artifact known as the Ark of the Covenant. This object made by Moses at Mount Sinai—part wooden-metal box and part golden statue—had the power to create "lightning" to kill people, and also to fly and lead people through the wilderness. The Ark of the Covenant suddenly disappears from the Bible record and what happened to it is not mentioned. Was it hidden in the underground passages of King Solomon's temple and later discovered by the Knights Templar? Was it taken through Egypt to Ethiopia as many Coptic Christians believe? Childress looks into hidden history, astonishing ancient technology, and a 3,000-year-old mystery that continues to fascinate millions of people today. Color section.
420 Pages. 6x9 Paperback. Illustrated. $22.00 Code: AOG

YETIS, SASQUATCH & HAIRY GIANTS
By David Hatcher Childress
Childress takes the reader on a fantastic journey across the Himalayas to Europe and North America in his quest for Yeti, Sasquatch and Hairy Giants. Childress begins with a discussion of giants and then tells of his own decades-long quest for the Yeti in Nepal, Sikkim, Bhutan and other areas of the Himalayas, and then proceeds to his research into Bigfoot, Sasquatch and Skunk Apes in North America. Chapters include: The Giants of Yore; Giants Among Us; Wildmen and Hairy Giants; The Call of the Yeti; Kanchenjunga Demons; The Yeti of Tibet, Mongolia & Russia; Bigfoot & the Grassman; Sasquatch Rules the Forest; Modern Sasquatch Accounts; more. Includes a 16-page color photo insert of astonishing photos!
360 pages. 5x9 Paperback. Illustrated. Bibliography. Index. $18.95. Code: YSHG

SECRETS OF THE HOLY LANCE
The Spear of Destiny in History & Legend
by Jerry E. Smith
Secrets of the Holy Lance traces the Spear from its possession by Constantine, Rome's first Christian Caesar, to Charlemagne's claim that with it he ruled the Holy Roman Empire by Divine Right, and on through two thousand years of kings and emperors, until it came within Hitler's grasp—and beyond! Did it rest for a while in Antarctic ice? Is it now hidden in Europe, awaiting the next person to claim its awesome power? Neither debunking nor worshiping, *Secrets of the Holy Lance* seeks to pierce the veil of myth and mystery around the Spear.
312 PAGES. 6x9 PAPERBACK. ILLUSTRATED. $16.95. CODE: SOHL

THE CRYSTAL SKULLS
Astonishing Portals to Man's Past
by David Hatcher Childress and Stephen S. Mehler
Childress introduces the technology and lore of crystals, and then plunges into the turbulent times of the Mexican Revolution form the backdrop for the rollicking adventures of Ambrose Bierce, the renowned journalist who went missing in the jungles in 1913, and F.A. Mitchell-Hedges, the notorious adventurer who emerged from the jungles with the most famous of the crystal skulls. Mehler shares his extensive knowledge of and experience with crystal skulls. Having been involved in the field since the 1980s, he has personally examined many of the most influential skulls, and has worked with the leaders in crystal skull research. Color section.
294 pages. 6x9 Paperback. Illustrated. $18.95. Code: CRSK

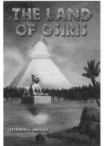

THE LAND OF OSIRIS
An Introduction to Khemitology
by Stephen S. Mehler
Was there an advanced prehistoric civilization in ancient Egypt? Were they the people who built the great pyramids and carved the Great Sphinx? Did the pyramids serve as energy devices and not as tombs for kings? Chapters include: Egyptology and Its Paradigms; Khemitology—New Paradigms; Asgat Nefer—The Harmony of Water; Khemit and the Myth of Atlantis; The Extraterrestrial Question; more. Color section.
272 PAGES. 6x9 PAPERBACK. ILLUSTRATED . $18.95. CODE: LOOS

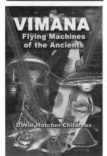

VIMANA:
Flying Machines of the Ancients
by David Hatcher Childress
According to early Sanskrit texts the ancients had several types of airships called vimanas. Like aircraft of today, vimanas were used to fly through the air from city to city; to conduct aerial surveys of uncharted lands; and as delivery vehicles for awesome weapons. David Hatcher Childress, popular *Lost Cities* author, takes us on an astounding investigation into tales of ancient flying machines. In his new book, packed with photos and diagrams, he consults ancient texts and modern stories and presents astonishing evidence that aircraft, similar to the ones we use today, were used thousands of years ago in India, Sumeria, China and other countries. Includes a 24-page color section.
408 Pages. 6x9 Paperback. Illustrated. $22.95. Code: VMA

THE LOST WORLD OF CHAM
The Trans-Pacific Voyages of the Champa
By David Hatcher Childress

The mysterious Cham, or Champa, peoples of Southeast Asia formed a megalith-building, seagoing empire that extended into Indonesia, Tonga, and beyond—a transoceanic power that reached Mexico and South America. The Champa maintained many ports in what is today Vietnam, Cambodia, and Indonesia and their ships plied the Indian Ocean and the Pacific, bringing Chinese, African and Indian traders to far off lands, including Olmec ports on the Pacific Coast of Central America. Topics include: Cham and Khem: Egyptian Influence on Cham; The Search for Metals; The Basalt City of Nan Madol; Elephants and Buddhists in North America; The Cham and Lake Titicaca; Easter Island and the Cham; the Magical Technology of the Cham; tons more. 24-page color section.
328 Pages. 6x9 Paperback. Illustrated. $22.00 Code: LPWC

ADVENTURES OF A HASHISH SMUGGLER
by Henri de Monfreid

Nobleman, writer, adventurer and inspiration for the swashbuckling gun runner in the *Adventures of Tintin*, Henri de Monfreid lived by his own account "a rich, restless, magnificent life" as one of the great travelers of his or any age. The son of a French artist who knew Paul Gaugin as a child, de Monfreid sought his fortune by becoming a collector and merchant of the fabled Persian Gulf pearls. He was then drawn into the shadowy world of arms trading, slavery, smuggling and drugs. Infamous as well as famous, his name is inextricably linked to the Red Sea and the raffish ports between Suez and Aden in the early years of the twentieth century. De Monfreid (1879 to 1974) had a long life of many adventures around the Horn of Africa where he dodged pirates as well as the authorities.
284 Pages. 6x9 Paperback. $16.95. Illustrated. Code AHS

NORTH CAUCASUS DOLMENS
In Search of Wonders
By Boris Loza, Ph.D.

Join Boris Loza as he travels to his ancestral homeland to uncover and explore dolmens firsthand. Throughout this journey, you will discover the often hidden, and surprisingly forbidden, perspective about the mysterious dolmens: their ancient powers of fertility, healing and spiritual connection. Chapters include: Ancient Mystic Megaliths; Who Built the Dolmens?; Why the Dolmens were Built; Asian Connection; Indian Connection; Greek Connection; Olmec and Maya Connection; Sun Worshippers; Dolmens and Archeoastronomy; Location of Dolmen Quarries; Hidden Power of Dolmens; and much more! Tons of Illustrations! A fascinating book of little-seen megaliths. Color section.
252 Pages. 5x9 Paperback. Illustrated. $24.00. Code NCD

THE ENCYCLOPEDIA OF MOON MYSTERIES
Secrets, Anomalies, Extraterrestrials and More
By Constance Victoria Briggs

Our moon is an enigma. The ancients viewed it as a light to guide them in the darkness, and a god to be worshipped. Some even believe that there are cities beneath the surface of the Moon. Did you know that: Aristotle and Plato wrote about a time when there was no Moon? Several of the NASA astronauts reported seeing UFOs while traveling to the Moon?; the Moon might be hollow?; Apollo 10 astronauts heard strange "space music" when traveling on the far side of the Moon?; strange and unexplained lights have been seen on the Moon for centuries?; there are said to be ruins of structures on the Moon?; there is an ancient tale that suggests that the first human was created on the Moon?; Tons more. Tons of illustrations with A to Z sections for easy reference and reading.
152 Pages. 7x10 Paperback. Illustrated. $19.95. Code: EOMM

TECHNOLOGY OF THE GODS
The Incredible Sciences of the Ancients
by David Hatcher Childress

Childress looks at the technology that was allegedly used in Atlantis and the theory that the Great Pyramid of Egypt was originally a gigantic power station. He examines tales of ancient flight and the technology that it involved; how the ancients used electricity; megalithic building techniques; the use of crystal lenses and the fire from the gods; evidence of various high tech weapons in the past, including atomic weapons; ancient metallurgy and heavy machinery; the role of modern inventors such as Nikola Tesla in bringing ancient technology back into modern use; impossible artifacts; and more.

356 pages. 6x9 Paperback. Illustrated. $16.95. code: TGOD

THE ANTI-GRAVITY HANDBOOK
edited by David Hatcher Childress

The new expanded compilation of material on Anti-Gravity, Free Energy, Flying Saucer Propulsion, UFOs, Suppressed Technology, NASA Cover-ups and more. Highly illustrated with patents, technical illustrations and photos. This revised and expanded edition has more material, including photos of Area 51, Nevada, the government's secret testing facility. This classic on weird science is back in a new format!

230 PAGES. 7X10 PAPERBACK. ILLUSTRATED. $16.95. CODE: AGH

ANTI–GRAVITY & THE WORLD GRID

Is the earth surrounded by an intricate electromagnetic grid network offering free energy? This compilation of material on ley lines and world power points contains chapters on the geography, mathematics, and light harmonics of the earth grid. Learn the purpose of ley lines and ancient megalithic structures located on the grid. Discover how the grid made the Philadelphia Experiment possible. Explore the Coral Castle and many other mysteries, including acoustic levitation, Tesla Shields and scalar wave weaponry. Browse through the section on anti-gravity patents, and research resources.

274 PAGES. 7X10 PAPERBACK. ILLUSTRATED. $14.95. CODE: AGW

ANTI–GRAVITY & THE UNIFIED FIELD
edited by David Hatcher Childress

Is Einstein's Unified Field Theory the answer to all of our energy problems? Explored in this compilation of material is how gravity, electricity and magnetism manifest from a unified field around us. Why artificial gravity is possible; secrets of UFO propulsion; free energy; Nikola Tesla and anti-gravity airships of the 20s and 30s; flying saucers as superconducting whirls of plasma; anti-mass generators; vortex propulsion; suppressed technology; government cover-ups; gravitational pulse drive; spacecraft & more.

240 PAGES. 7X10 PAPERBACK. ILLUSTRATED. $14.95. CODE: AGU

THE TIME TRAVEL HANDBOOK
A Manual of Practical Teleportation & Time Travel
edited by David Hatcher Childress

The Time Travel Handbook takes the reader beyond the government experiments and deep into the uncharted territory of early time travellers such as Nikola Tesla and Guglielmo Marconi and their alleged time travel experiments, as well as the Wilson Brothers of EMI and their connection to the Philadelphia Experiment—the U.S. Navy's forays into invisibility, time travel, and teleportation. Childress looks into the claims of time travelling individuals, and investigates the unusual claim that the pyramids on Mars were built in the future and sent back in time. A highly visual, large format book, with patents, photos and schematics. Be the first on your block to build your own time travel device!

316 PAGES. 7X10 PAPERBACK. ILLUSTRATED. $16.95. CODE: TTH

ANCIENT ALIENS ON THE MOON
By Mike Bara
What did NASA find in their explorations of the solar system that they may have kept from the general public? How ancient really are these ruins on the Moon? Using official NASA and Russian photos of the Moon, Bara looks at vast cityscapes and domes in the Sinus Medii region as well as glass domes in the Crisium region. Bara also takes a detailed look at the mission of Apollo 17 and the case that this was a salvage mission, primarily concerned with investigating an opening into a massive hexagonal ruin near the landing site. Chapters include: The History of Lunar Anomalies; The Early 20th Century; Sinus Medii; To the Moon Alice!; Mare Crisium; Yes, Virginia, We Really Went to the Moon; Apollo 17; more. Tons of photos of the Moon examined for possible structures and other anomalies.
248 Pages. 6x9 Paperback. Illustrated.. $19.95. Code: AAOM

ANCIENT ALIENS ON MARS
By Mike Bara
Bara brings us this lavishly illustrated volume on alien structures on Mars. Was there once a vast, technologically advanced civilization on Mars, and did it leave evidence of its existence behind for humans to find eons later? Did these advanced extraterrestrial visitors vanish in a solar system wide cataclysm of their own making, only to make their way to Earth and start anew? Was Mars once as lush and green as the Earth, and teeming with life? Chapters include: War of the Worlds; The Mars Tidal Model; The Death of Mars; Cydonia and the Face on Mars; The Monuments of Mars; The Search for Life on Mars; The True Colors of Mars and The Pathfinder Sphinx; more. Color section.
252 Pages. 6x9 Paperback. Illustrated. $19.95. Code: AMAR

ANCIENT ALIENS ON MARS II
By Mike Bara
Using data acquired from sophisticated new scientific instruments like the Mars Odyssey THEMIS infrared imager, Bara shows that the region of Cydonia overlays a vast underground city full of enormous structures and devices that may still be operating. He peels back the layers of mystery to show images of tunnel systems, temples and ruins, and exposes the sophisticated NASA conspiracy designed to hide them. Bara also tackles the enigma of Mars' hollowed out moon Phobos, and exposes evidence that it is artificial. Long-held myths about Mars, including claims that it is protected by a sophisticated UFO defense system, are examined. Data from the Mars rovers Spirit, Opportunity and Curiosity are examined; everything from fossilized plants to mechanical debris is exposed in images taken directly from NASA's own archives.
294 Pages. 6x9 Paperback. Illustrated. $19.95. Code: AAM2

ANCIENT TECHNOLOGY IN PERU & BOLIVIA
By David Hatcher Childress
Childress speculates on the existence of a sunken city in Lake Titicaca and reveals new evidence that the Sumerians may have arrived in South America 4,000 years ago. He demonstrates that the use of "keystone cuts" with metal clamps poured into them to secure megalithic construction was an advanced technology used all over the world, from the Andes to Egypt, Greece and Southeast Asia. He maintains that only power tools could have made the intricate articulation and drill holes found in extremely hard granite and basalt blocks in Bolivia and Peru, and that the megalith builders had to have had advanced methods for moving and stacking gigantic blocks of stone, some weighing over 100 tons.
340 Pages. 6x9 Paperback. Illustrated.. $19.95 Code: ATP

BIGFOOT NATION
A History of Sasquatch in North America
By David Hatcher Childress
Childress takes a deep look at Bigfoot Nation—the real world of bigfoot around us in the United States and Canada. Whether real or imagined, that bigfoot has made his way into the American psyche cannot be denied. He appears in television commercials, movies, and on roadside billboards. Bigfoot is everywhere, with actors portraying him in variously believable performances and it has become the popular notion that bigfoot is both dangerous and horny. Indeed, bigfoot is out there stalking lovers' lanes and is even more lonely than those frightened teenagers that he sometimes interrupts. Bigfoot, tall and strong as he is, makes a poor leading man in the movies with his awkward personality and typically anti-social behavior. Includes 16-pages of color photos that document Bigfoot Nation!
320 Pages. 6x9 Paperback. Illustrated. $22.00. Code: BGN

MEN & GODS IN MONGOLIA
by Henning Haslund
Haslund takes us to the lost city of Karakota in the Gobi desert. We meet the Bodgo Gegen, a god-king in Mongolia similar to the Dalai Lama of Tibet. We meet Dambin Jansang, the dreaded warlord of the "Black Gobi." Haslund and companions journey across the Gobi desert by camel caravan; are kidnapped and held for ransom; withness initiation into Shamanic societies; meet reincarnated warlords; and experience the violent birth of "modern" Mongolia.
358 Pages. 6x9 Paperback. Illustrated. $18.95. Code: MGM

PROJECT MK-ULTRA
AND MIND CONTROL TECHNOLOGY
By Axel Balthazar
This book is a compilation of the government's documentation on MK-Ultra, the CIA's mind control experimentation on unwitting human subjects, as well as over 150 patents pertaining to artificial telepathy (voice-to-skull technology), behavior modification through radio frequencies, directed energy weapons, electronic monitoring, implantable nanotechnology, brain wave manipulation, nervous system manipulation, neuroweapons, psychological warfare, satellite terrorism, subliminal messaging, and more. A must-have reference guide for targeted individuals and anyone interested in the subject of mind control technology.
384 pages. 7x10 Paperback. Illustrated. $19.95. Code: PMK

LIQUID CONSPIRACY 2:
The CIA, MI6 & Big Pharma's War on Psychedelics
By Xaviant Haze
Underground author Xaviant Haze looks into the CIA and its use of LSD as a mind control drug; at one point every CIA officer had to take the drug and endure mind control tests and interrogations to see if the drug worked as a "truth serum." Chapters include: The Pioneers of Psychedelia; The United Kingdom Mellows Out: The MI5, MDMA and LSD; Taking it to the Streets: LSD becomes Acid; Great Works of Art Inspired and Influenced by Acid; Scapolamine: The CIA's Ultimate Truth Serum; Mind Control, the Death of Music and the Meltdown of the Masses; Big Pharma's War on Psychedelics; The Healing Powers of Psychedelic Medicine; tons more.
240 pages. 6x9 Paperback. Illustrated. $19.95. Code: LQC2

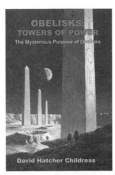

OBELISKS: TOWERS OF POWER
The Mysterious Purpose of Obelisks
By David Hatcher Childress

Some obelisks weigh over 500 tons and are massive blocks of polished granite that would be extremely difficult to quarry and erect even with modern equipment. Why did ancient civilizations in Egypt, Ethiopia and elsewhere undertake the massive enterprise it would have been to erect a single obelisk, much less dozens of them? Were they energy towers that could receive or transmit energy? With discussions on Tesla's wireless power, and the use of obelisks as gigantic acupuncture needles for earth, Chapters include: Megaliths Around the World and their Purpose; The Crystal Towers of Egypt; The Obelisks of Ethiopia; Obelisks in Europe and Asia; Mysterious Obelisks in the Americas; The Terrible Crystal Towers of Atlantis; Tesla's Wireless Power Distribution System; Obelisks on the Moon; more. 8-page color section.
336 Pages. 6x9 Paperback. Illustrated. $22.00 Code: OBK

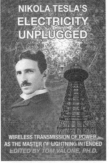

NIKOLA TESLA'S ELECTRICITY UNPLUGGED
Wireless Transmission of Power as the Master of Lightning Intended
Edited by Tom Valone, Ph.D.

The immense genius of Tesla resulted from his ability to see an invention in 3-D, from every angle, within his mind before it was easily built. Tesla's inventions were complete down to dimensions and part sizes in his visionary process. Tesla would envision his electromagnetic devices as he stared into the sky, or into a corner of his laboratory. His inventions on rotating magnetic fields, creating AC current as we know it today, have changed the world—yet most people have never heard of this great inventor. Includes: Tesla's fantastic vision of the future, his wireless transmission of power, Tesla's Magnifying Transmitter, the testing and building of his towers for wireless power, tons more. The genius of Nikola Tesla is being realized by millions all over the world!
464 pages. 6x9 Paperback. Illustrated. Index. $21.95 Code: NTEU

THE TESLA PAPERS
Nikola Tesla on Free Energy & Wireless Transmission of Power
by Nikola Tesla, edited by David Hatcher Childress

David Hatcher Childress takes us into the incredible world of Nikola Tesla and his amazing inventions. Tesla's fantastic vision of the future, including wireless power, anti-gravity, free energy and highly advanced solar power. Also included are some of the papers, patents and material collected on Tesla at the Colorado Springs Tesla Symposiums, including papers on: •The Secret History of Wireless Transmission •Tesla and the Magnifying Transmitter •Design and Construction of a Half-Wave Tesla Coil •Electrostatics: A Key to Free Energy •Progress in Zero-Point Energy Research •Electromagnetic Energy from Antennas to Atoms
325 PAGES. 8x10 PAPERBACK. ILLUSTRATED. $16.95. CODE: TTP

ROBOT ZOMBIES
Transhumanism and the Robot Revolution
By Xaviant Haze and Estrella Eguino,

Technology is growing exponentially and the moment when it merges with the human mind, called "The Singularity," is visible in our imminent future. Science and technology are pushing forward, transforming life as we know it—perhaps even giving humans a shot at immortality. This book examines the history and future of robotics, artificial intelligence, zombies and a Transhumanist utopia/dystopia integrating man with machine. Chapters include: Love, Sex and Compassion—Android Style; Humans Aren't Working Like They Used To; Skynet Rises; Blueprints for Transhumans; Kurzweil's Quest; Nanotech Dreams; Zombies Among Us; Cyborgs (Cylons) in Space; Awakening the Human; more. Color Section.
180 Pages. 6x9 Paperback. Illustrated. $16.95. Code: RBTZ

ORDER FORM

**10% Discount
When You Order
3 or More Items!**

One Adventure Place
P.O. Box 74
Kempton, Illinois 60946
United States of America
Tel.: 815-253-6390 • Fax: 815-253-6300
Email: auphq@frontiernet.net
http://www.adventuresunlimitedpress.com

ORDERING INSTRUCTIONS

✓ Remit by USD$ Check, Money Order or Credit Card
✓ Visa, Master Card, Discover & AmEx Accepted
✓ Paypal Payments Can Be Made To:

    info@wexclub.com

✓ Prices May Change Without Notice
✓ 10% Discount for 3 or More Items

SHIPPING CHARGES

United States

✓ Postal Book Rate { $4.50 First Item
    50¢ Each Additional Item
✓ POSTAL BOOK RATE Cannot Be Tracked!
    Not responsible for non-delivery.
✓ Priority Mail { $7.00 First Item
    $2.00 Each Additional Item
✓ UPS { $9.00 First Item (Minimum 5 Books)
    $1.50 Each Additional Item
NOTE: UPS Delivery Available to Mainland USA Only

Canada

✓ Postal Air Mail { $19.00 First Item
    $3.00 Each Additional Item
✓ Personal Checks or Bank Drafts MUST BE

    US$ and Drawn on a US Bank

✓ Canadian Postal Money Orders OK

✓ Payment MUST BE US$

All Other Countries

✓ Sorry, No Surface Delivery!

✓ Postal Air Mail { $19.00 First Item
    $7.00 Each Additional Item

✓ Checks and Money Orders MUST BE US$
    and Drawn on a US Bank or branch.

✓ Paypal Payments Can Be Made in US$ To:
    info@wexclub.com

SPECIAL NOTES

✓ RETAILERS: Standard Discounts Available
✓ BACKORDERS: We Backorder all Out-of-
Stock Items Unless Otherwise Requested

✓ PRO FORMA INVOICES: Available on Request
✓ DVD Return Policy: Replace defective DVDs only
ORDER ONLINE AT: www.adventuresunlimitedpress.com

**10% Discount When You Order
3 or More Items!**

Please check: ✓

☐ This is my first order   ☐ I have ordered before

Name			
Address			
City			
State/Province		Postal Code	
Country			
Phone: Day		Evening	
Fax		Email	

Item Code	Item Description	Qty	Total

Please check: ✓

Subtotal ▸

Less Discount-10% for 3 or more items ▸

☐ Postal-Surface   Balance ▸

☐ Postal-Air Mail Illinois Residents 6.25% Sales Tax ▸
(Priority in USA)   Previous Credit ▸

☐ UPS   Shipping ▸
(Mainland USA only) Total (check/MO in USD$ only) ▸

☐ Visa/MasterCard/Discover/American Express

Card Number:

Expiration Date: Security Code:

✓ SEND A CATALOG TO A FRIEND: